The reason of rules

The reason of rules
Constitutional political economy

GEOFFREY BRENNAN
Australian National University

JAMES M. BUCHANAN
George Mason University

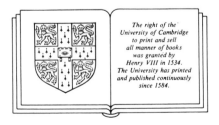

The right of the
University of Cambridge
to print and sell
all manner of books
was granted by
Henry VIII in 1534.
The University has printed
and published continuously
since 1584.

CAMBRIDGE UNIVERSITY PRESS

Cambridge
London   New York   New Rochelle
Melbourne   Sydney

Published by the Press Syndicate of the University of Cambridge
The Pitt Building, Trumpington Street, Cambridge CB2 1RP
32 East 57th Street, New York, NY 10022, USA
10 Stamford Road, Oakleigh, Melbourne 3166, Australia

First published 1985

Printed in the United States of America

Library of Congress Cataloging in Publication Data
Brennan, H. Geoffrey, 1944–
The reason of rules.
1. Economics – Political aspects. 2. Social contract.
3. Constitutional law. I. Buchanan, James M. II. Title.
III. Title: Constitutional political economy.
HB73.B74 1985   338.9   85-4178
ISBN 0 521 25655 0

Contents

v

Preface

Anglo-American jurisprudence emphasizes the rule of reason; it grossly neglects the reason of rules. We play socioeconomic−legal−political games that can be described empirically only by their rules. But most of us play without *an understanding or appreciation of* the rules, how they came into being, how they are enforced, how they can be changed, and, most important, how they can be normatively evaluated. Basic "constitutional illiteracy" extends to and includes both the learned and the lay. We note with a mixture of admiration and envy those clever strategists who manipulate existing rules to their own advantage. It is these persons in the role of spivs rather than the sages that all too many emulate. Intelligence abounds, but wisdom seems increasingly scarce.

Our hypothesis is corroborated by the veneration Americans accord their Founding Fathers. James Madison, Benjamin Franklin, Thomas Jefferson, and their peers are distinguished by their essential understanding of the reason of rules in political order, an understanding they implanted in the constitutional documents, the "sacred" texts that have, indeed, worked their influence through two centuries. The wisdom and understanding of the Founders have been seriously eroded in our time. The deterioration of the social−intellectual−philosophical capital of Western civil order is now widely, if only intuitively, sensed.

At the most fundamental level, rules find their reason in the never ending desire of people to live together in peace and harmony, without the continuing Hobbesian war of each against all. How can social order be established and preserved? All social science and philosophy must address this question, either directly or indirectly.

In part, the relative neglect of the question in its explicit form stems from the absence of a clearly defined answer. When we recognize that man's natural proclivity is to pursue his own interests and that different persons' interests almost inevitably come into conflict, it is all too easy to despair. Any social order seems to rest on extremely fragile foundations. Must life tend to be either "nasty, brutish, and short" in anarchy or "nasty, brutish, and slavish" under Leviathan?

Two broadly defined escape routes have offered hope to scholars and citizens through the ages. One of them is man's capacity for moral improvement. People may, in a time to be, come to love one another. Much energy has been expended in promoting this objective. The observed record of success is dubious, although we do not want here to judge such effort unworthy or unnecessary.

The second possible avenue of escape from the "social dilemma" does not require that people become "better" in some basic moral sense. This approach starts with the empirical realities of persons as they exist, moral warts and all. These realities, summarized somewhat unsatisfactorily in the catchall term "human nature," limit the attainable states of social harmony. But even within such constraints, hope emerges for sustainable social order through the appropriate design, construction, and maintenance of *rules* that set limits on the way in which each person is allowed to order his conduct toward others.

The notion that rules may substitute for morals has been familiar to economists and philosophers at least since Adam Smith. And, of course, the great intellectual discovery of the eighteenth century was the spontaneous order of the market, the discovery that within an appropriate structure of rules ("laws and institutions" in Adam Smith's phraseology), individuals in following their own interests can further the interests of others. The result is the great network of social coordination — refined and extended to the boundaries of the division of labor — that even after centuries defies the imagination when evaluated as a cooperative enterprise. The cooperation of agents in a market, however, requires neither that such agents understand the structure nor that they transcend ordinary precepts of morality in their behavior. What it does require is an appropriate "constitutional context" — a proper structure of rules, along with some arrangements for their enforcement.

All of this was once the centerpiece of "political economy," and even today economics textbooks retain vestiges of such principles. But at one time an economist was literally defined as a person who "knows how markets work," with "work" being understood in terms of the coordination of individual behavior through the institutional structure. Since the early years of this century, however, professional economists have shifted their attention. They have become preoccupied with predicting the effects of exogenous changes on the observable and measurable aspects of market outcomes (price, wage rates, quantities, etc.) and with elaborating the logical implications of alternative assumptions (or alternative "models"). With this shift of attention, modern economists seem to have all but lost the earlier understanding, which was, perhaps, their primary raison d'être in any "social" sense.

In public-choice theory, which applies the techniques and analytic apparatus of modern economics to the study of political processes, a similar divergence in emphasis is distinguishable. Some modern scholars view public-choice theory as offering a "pure science" of politics that is fully analogous to the "science" of markets. The objective is to derive testable hypotheses about the effects of specified changes in basic parameters on observed political results. Still other public-choice (social-choice) theorists concern themselves with analytic esoterica in the modeling of alternative political arrangements. The third strand of research activity within public choice, and the strand with which we have been personally most involved, has more in common with the earlier tradition in "political economy." The objective here is to understand the workings of alternative political institutions so that choices among such institutions (or structures of rules) can be more fully informed. We have called this research program "constitutional political economy," both in our subtitle for this book and in other works. Broadly defined, the methodology of constitutional political economy is the subject matter of this book.

This research program is not new for either of us. We have, jointly, separately, and severally, in bits and pieces, here and there, made previous attempts to shore up constitutional understanding. Specifically, we have made some start at analyzing how rules of political order work, how such rules might be chosen, and how normative criteria for such choices might be established. We have also, particularly in works written in the early 1980s, attempted to analyze the basic logic of rules, to indicate why rules or institutions rather than outcomes should be the central focus of inquiry. As it turns out, this sort of analysis, which we had thought to be almost universally understood, has proved surprisingly controversial. Our experience in attempting to persuade others, both in the academy and beyond, to accept the results of analysis of the more sophisticated and complex questions of constitutional design has generated a developing conviction that the intellectual problem lies at the deepest level of the mental process. Without a shared "constitutional mentality," without some initial common ground from which discourse can proceed, all argument on design comes to naught. Persons must be cognizant of the *reason* of rules before they can enter into dialogues devoted to questions concerning choices among rules.

Since we are ourselves professional economists, we have been particularly mystified by the reluctance of our profession to adopt what we have called the constitutional perspective. Economists in this century have been greatly concerned with "market failure," which was the central focus of the theoretical welfare economists that dominated economic thought during the middle decades of the century. This market-failure emphasis extended to both micro- and macrolevels of analysis. Scholars working at either of these levels showed no reluctance in proffering advice to governments on detailed market correctives and macroeconomic management. In retrospect, post–public choice, it seems strange that these scholars so rarely showed a willingness to apply their analytic apparatus to institutions other than the market; they paid almost no attention to politics and political institutions. Once a policy recommendation seemed to have emerged from their market-failure analytics, there was no subsequent analysis aimed at proving that persons in their political roles, as either principals or agents, would somehow behave as the economists' precepts dictated. Implicitly, economists seemed locked into the presumption that political authority is vested in a group of moral superpersons, whose behavior might be described by an appropriately constrained social welfare function. Initial cursory attempts by a few public-choice pioneers to inject a bit of practical realism into our models of individual behavior in politics were subjected to charges of ideological bias. The myth of the benign despot seems to have considerable staying power, a phenomenon that we examine specifically in Chapter 3.

In its most fundamental aspects, the difference between the constitutionalist and nonconstitutionalist perspectives involves a difference in man's vision of himself as a conscious being interacting with others in a social order. Our interests are limited by our presupposition that persons must be evaluated as moral equals. In our research program, the constitutionalist perspective is necessarily contractarian, a point that is the subject matter of Chapter 2.

The discussion in this book can be divided into four parts. The first four chapters cover general issues in any analysis of rules. Chapter 1 makes the basic distinction between endstates, or outcomes, emergent from behavior within rules and the rules themselves. We attempt to indicate why our emphasis on rules is important by introducing several independent justifications. As already noted, Chapter 2 discusses the properties of the normative stance usually labeled "contractarian." As also noted, Chapter 3 embodies our attempt to understand the opposition to a constitutional approach. Chapter 4 is concerned with a methodological dimension of the distinction between in-period and constitutional choice – a widely overlooked dimension that brings our work more closely into line with that of the classical political economists. Specifically, we argue that the behavioral assumptions appropriate for an analysis of rules may be different from those relevant to making predictions about outcomes generated under well-defined rules.

Chapters 5 and 6 deal with the temporal dimension of choice in the private — as distinct from the collective — choice setting. The object is to show that individuals will rationally discount the future more heavily in the collective-choice context — a fact that provides a distinct reason for rules in collective-choice settings. The general abstract argument of Chapter 5 is developed in Chapter 6 by appeal to three modern examples. The analysis of "politics without rules" through these examples establishes general support for the earlier analytic argument.

Chapters 7 and 8 deal with the connection between rules and "justice," variously construed. Chapter 7 offers an interpretation of the notion of justice that depends on the prior existence of rule-bound behavior. To the extent that justice is valued, justice so understood provides a reason for rules. In Chapter 8 we attend to the question of distributive justice. The focus is on the workings of "politics without rules" in the attempted implementation of a norm for distributive justice, as opposed to the more familiar discussion devoted to comparisons of alternative imaginable "distributions."

The book concludes with Chapter 9, which stands apart from the rest of the discussion. We could properly be accused of naïveté if we failed to address the critical issue of implementation. Is constitutional change possible in democracy? Clearly, *no*, if there is widespread ignorance about the reason of rules. But even with some requisite constitutional wisdom, how can reform surmount identifiable self-interest? Cassandra looks over our shoulders here, but our whole effort, in this book and elsewhere, testifies to our faith that we can, as participants in the ongoing academic dialogue and ultimately as citizens, *improve* the rules of the game we play.

As noted, part of the motivation for our exercise in this book lies in the reaction our previous work encountered — among sympathizers and antagonists alike. Much of that reaction was based, we believe, on a major misunderstanding — a failure to grasp what we had attempted to do. Whether we have been more successful in the present effort only our readers can decide. The only point to be made here is that in writing this book, we have been more than usually dependent on our critics. In this connection, we should express particular gratitude to Richard Musgrave and Jules Coleman, who paid us the greatest possible academic compliment — that of taking our work seriously. Among our immediate colleagues, Dwight Lee contributed to some of the ideas expressed in the chapters on politics and time, and Loren Lomasky, always a stimulating presence, provided valued comments on earlier versions of Chapters 6 and 7. Viktor Vanberg's comments on Chapter 1 helped us avoid ambiguities, and Dennis Mueller's comments on Chapter 7 were helpful. Robert Tollison's several notes helped us improve the whole manuscript.

This book, like its predecessor *The Power to Tax* and many shorter works, is a genuinely joint product of both authors. The labor had to be divided, however, and first-draft responsibility parceled out. To Brennan fell the task of initially drafting Chapters 1, 4, 7, and 8; to Buchanan the remainder, Chapters 2, 3, 5, 6, and 9. Some of the material in Buchanan's chapters in particular was originally presented in lectures at Liberty Fund conferences at Snowbird, Utah, in 1981 and at Oxford, England, in 1982.

We have been assisted in our efforts directly by the Center for Study of Public Choice, George Mason University, and indirectly by those who have generously supported the center's program. For the more inclusive project on "constitutional political economy" of which this book is only a part, we gratefully acknowledge the specific support of the Foundation for Research in Economics and Education, Los Angeles.

In the emerging Buchanan tradition, we must once again thank Betty Tillman for putting the package together. Her effort was more than usually noble, since it occurred in the wake of a major move that involved the entire Public Choice Center, a move she orchestrated virtually unaided. Her extraordinary dedication and unfailing cheerfulness, which have been characteristic for more than two decades, have continually surprised us and merit our continuing gratitude.

CHAPTER 1

The constitutional imperative

I. Introduction

There is something profoundly unsatisfactory about economists' introducing their subject matter by reference to the Robinson Crusoe who faces an "economic problem" because he must decide how to allocate his scarce resources (including time) among competing uses. With this introduction, it becomes far too easy to slip from the Crusoe setting into one in which "society" as such also faces the "economic problem" and to jump, almost inadvertently, from analyses of individual utility maximization to direct concern with maximization of value for society.

What is left out in such a pedogogical sequence is the *interaction* among separate individuals who make up a society. Individuals face choices in a social setting in which the existence and behavior of other persons, along with the institutions that constrain their behavior, are much more important than the physical constraints of nature. Economics is, or should be, about individual behavior in society.

Such behavior is not necessarily "social" in the sense that individuals recognize the existence of reciprocal influence among the actions of directly interacting parties. Individual behavior in large modern societies may be totally impersonal, as exemplified in the idealized models of competitive markets. In the limiting case, all participants respond to exogenously determined parameters: No person exercises any direct influence on another. The outcomes of the complex interdependence of all actors are not available as objects of choice for any actor.

In the limiting case, or in more general settings where at least some part of behavior is explicitly "social," the *rules* that coordinate the actions of individuals are important and are crucial to any understanding of the interdependence process. The same individuals, with the same motivations and capacities, will interact to generate quite different aggregate outcomes under differing sets of rules, with quite different implications for the well-being of every participant. The allocation of an individual's time and energy will be different in a setting where rewards are related to performance and in a setting where rewards are determined by other criteria. At least since the

1

eighteenth century, and notably since Adam Smith, the influence of rules (Smith's term was "laws and institutions") on social outcomes has been understood, and this relationship has provided the basis for a central theme in economics and political economy, particularly as derived from their classical foundations.

If rules influence outcomes and if some outcomes are "better" than others, it follows that to the extent that rules can be chosen, the study and analysis of comparative rules and institutions become proper objects of our attention. Without an understanding of how the individuals who make up a social order interact, and how different sets of rules affect these interactions, it is impossible for participants to make informed changes in existing rules or even to behave prudently with respect to the preservation of those rules that have proved essential to the tolerably efficient functioning of the society as such.

What advice can we offer ourselves in our own societies, standing as we do with the benefits of cooperation and the prospects of conflict on either hand? What aspects of our social life should we discard? Where are there "rules of social order" – institutional arrangements governing our interactions – that lead us to affect one another adversely? Where are there forces for harmony that can be mobilized? What rules – and what institutions – should we be struggling to preserve?

These questions represent the area of inquiry we term "constitutional political economy" (in the spirit of the classical political economists, for whom such questions were also central). They are important questions even if they are so widely ignored in modern discourse. And they are not asked in a total intellectual analytic vacuum. They have, indeed, occupied some of the greatest minds in the Western tradition. Unfortunately, much of the accumulated wisdom seems to have fallen between the cracks. Such questions are often considered to be merely ideological, so that the answers are simply matters of opinion on which one view is about as good as any other. There is, to be sure, a considerable range of permissible disagreement. But there is also a procedure for asking the questions and a method of analysis that sets the terms within which debate can range.

The questions themselves, the proper procedures for asking them, the relevant analytic method – these make up the agenda for this book. Our aim in this opening chapter is to set the stage – to hammer in a few pegs on which we can subsequently throw various hats. Specifically, we shall offer a characterization of various sorts of interactions, initially in abstract terms. We shall indicate, again abstractly, the ways in which rules and institutions are relevant to the nature of the interactions that

B

	I 6,6	II 0,10
A	III 10,0	IV 1,1

Matrix 1.1

prevail. We shall then relate the various interaction types to different social contexts with which they are often associated. Finally, we shall briefly discuss rules in general and relate some of the insights gained thereby to the social–political–economic setting, which is, of course, our central concern.

II. Reasons for rules

The title of this book is *The Reason of Rules*, and we shall discuss many reasons in detail as we proceed. But first, the most fundamental of all reasons must be discussed, even though it has been elaborated in some detail in other works.[1] We require rules in society because, without them, life would indeed be "solitary, poore, nasty, brutish, and short," as Thomas Hobbes told us more than three centuries ago.[2] Only the romantic anarchist thinks there is a "natural harmony" among persons that will eliminate all conflict in the absence of rules. We require rules for living together for the simple reason that without them we would surely fight. We would fight because the object of desire for one individual would be claimed by another. Rules define the private spaces within which each of us can carry on our own activities.

Perhaps the best way, and one of the most familiar ways, of illustrating this potential for conflict among persons and the potential means of resolving it is the classic prisoners' dilemma. Consider Matrix 1.1, in which the numbers in each cell represent positively valued payoffs to each of two persons, A and B, with the left-hand number in each cell indicating the payoff to A and the right-hand number that to B. Note

[1] See, in particular, James M. Buchanan, *The Limits of Liberty* (University of Chicago Press, 1975).
[2] Thomas Hobbes, *Leviathan* (1651) (New York: Everyman Edition, 1943).

that there is both row and column dominance. That is to say, if there is only one play of the game, A, who chooses between rows, will select row 2, independently of his prediction as to how B will behave. Similarly, B, who chooses between columns, will select column 2. As a result of this independent behavior, the "solution" lies in cell IV. As the payoffs indicate, however, *both* persons would do better if they chose row 1 and column 1, with the solution in cell I. Unless there is some rule or convention that dictates such action, however, privately rational and utility-maximizing behavior will guarantee the result in cell IV. There is, in this setting, a clear and simple message. For the community of persons involved in this interaction, there is a need for a rule, a socially binding norm that will prevent the individuals from behaving so as to end up with the outcome depicted in cell IV, an outcome that neither desires.

Several points worth noting emerge from this simple illustration. First, as indicated earlier, neither A nor B can individually determine the outcome of the social interaction. The outcome emerges from the behavior of *both* parties, whether this behavior is described as individual expected utility maximizing without rules or as adherence to some rule or convention.

Second, the potentiality for agreement on some rule or convention exists so long as the structure of the interaction remains as depicted in the matrix. That is to say, the "game" need not be symmetric in its payoffs, as shown. All that is required is that the ordinal rankings of the cells be the same as depicted for each of the parties involved. So long as A ranks the cells III, I, IV, II, and B ranks them II, I, IV, III, the results will hold. Hence, we could, if desired, multiply the numbers for, say, A by a factor of 100, while holding the numbers for B as indicated, without modifying the basic structure of the interaction.

Third, even this simple illustration suggests the problem of enforcibility of a rule despite the potential for general agreement on its desirability. Suppose that A and B agree to choose row 1 and column 1, respectively, so generating an expected outcome in cell I. If A expects B to abide by the agreement, however, A can himself secure a higher payoff by choosing row 2 rather than row 1, as agreed. Similarly, B can choose column 2 and improve his position if he expects A to choose row 1. Any rule, therefore, that will ensure a higher overall payoff, if respected by all persons, is vulnerable to violation motivated by privately rational behavior on the part of some or all parties to an interaction. It is not as if a potential violator must be deviant or irrational in his behavior. Indeed, this supposition might almost be reversed. In the absence of effective enforcement procedures, adherence to rules rather than departure from them requires that individuals forswear expected utility maximization, at least as this behavioral proposition is usually formulated in modern economic theory.

The prisoners' dilemma interaction is highly simplified, but it does, we suggest, contain in its structure most of the elements required for an understanding of the central problems of social order, those of reconciling the behavior of separately motivated persons so as to generate patterns of outcomes that are tolerable to all participants. Our colleague, Gordon Tullock, aptly titled his book on the subject *The Social Dilemma*,[3] thereby suggesting the ubiquity of the problem. When generalized, the dilemma will, of course, take on highly complex structural characteristics. As we extend the analysis to include many persons, who may act separately, in groups, or as a collective unit through the agencies of government, and many choice options, including several levels of choice-making, there is almost no limit to the number of interesting interaction settings that might be examined.

Our purpose in this book is not, however, to model even a small subset of such interactions. From here on in, we shall take as our point of departure an understanding of the generalized dilemma that suggests the overall desirability of rules or sets of rules that define the appropriate constraints on individual, group, and collective behavior. In the remaining parts of this chapter, we shall isolate attributes of rules in several familiar interactions as a means of introducing the discussion of rules in the sociopolitical context.

III.   Rules of games

When the word "rules" is mentioned, perhaps the most familiar association is with "games." And it will be useful to discuss rules in ordinary games — parlor games such as bridge, or sports such as tennis or basketball. All games have rules that define the parameters within which play takes place — the actions allowed by the players, the equipment used, the means of settling disputes, the way in which the winner is determined, and so on.

In discussing ordinary games, we have little or no difficulty in distinguishing between the *rules* of the game as such and *plays* of the game within these rules. Play takes place within the rules, but play itself does not constitute part of the rules. Rules provide the framework for the playing of the game, and many different patterns of play may take

---

[3] Gordon Tullock, *The Social Dilemma* (Blacksburg, Va.: University Publications, 1974).

place within given rules. By contrast, a particular play of the game is determinate or closed. Indeed, it is confusing that in common usage we use the word "game" to refer both to the structure of the rules (e.g., "basketball is a *game*") and to the play within the rules (e.g., "the Lakers beat the Celtics in last night's *game*").

In a sociopolitical context, the same distinctions apply between rules of social interaction and the patterns of behavior that take place within those rules. The distinction here is often more difficult to make than in ordinary games, and the discussion of the latter is helpful in precisely this respect. The validity of the distinction between rules and behavior within rules is general, however, over all interaction settings.

The ordinary game setting also facilitates discussion of a related but separate distinction between the choice of a strategy of play within a set of defined rules and the choice of the rules themselves. The choice of a group of potential poker players between stud and draw poker is quite different from the choice of a single player, under stud poker rules, between folding or staying in for an extra card.

The corresponding distinction in the sociopolitical context must be emphasized. It is necessary to separate the process through which the rules are determined from the process through which particular actions within those rules are chosen. Again, however, the distinction is somewhat more difficult to draw in the social setting because of the complex interdependencies between the rules that define the constraints on private behavior and the rules that define the constraints on the political agents who may engage in activities involving changes in the first set of rules. That is to say, legislative majorities may be acting *within the rules* (the political constitution) that constrain their own behavior in *changing the rules* that constrain the behavior of persons in their private capacities. One must be careful to make the distinction between a choice among rules and a choice among strategies within rules applicable to the situation confronted by a well-defined decision-making unit. For example, if a property rule allows us to burn brush on our own land, we act within the rules when we decide to burn a pile of brush on a particular day. A legislative enactment outlawing brush burning amounts to a change in the rules that we, as private landowners, follow. But the legislature, in passing this regulation, acts within its own rules, consisting, say, of simple majority voting. A primary advantage of beginning our discussion with familiar ordinary games is that the two levels of choice are intuitively clear.

The treatment of rules in ordinary games may be misleading in certain respects. Ordinary games are designed to make play within the rules interesting. That is, play as such is one objective shared by all potential participants. The basic dilemma that we introduced earlier, in which rules are desired because they lead to avoidance of unwanted outcomes, tends to be obscured in the treatment of ordinary games.

As we shift attention to the settings for sociopolitical interactions, there need be nothing analogous to the enjoyment of play as such, and the payoffs to individual players need not be designed as counters for the purpose of making the activity interesting. There need be no shared objective in sociopolitical rules. Individuals are recognized to possess their own privately determined objectives, their own life plans, and these need not be common to all persons. In this setting, rules have the function of facilitating interactions among persons who may desire quite different things. To discuss this feature, it is best to shift to an alternative framework.

IV. Rules of the road

Rules of the road, another familiar usage of the terms here, are not designed and/or did not evolve on the basis of any specification of the objectives of persons who are road users. Road users have widely varying purposes — business, pleasure, or some combination — which dictate many varieties of route, speed, and type of vehicle. Rules of the road serve the function of allowing persons to pursue their separate and independent courses, which may conflict in the absence of such rules. These rules do not imply that the objectives of users be reduced to a single counter, analogous to "winning" in ordinary games.

Road rules draw another feature to our attention. The efficacy of a set of rules does not depend on any matching of skill levels among those who use the facility. A set of rules may be preferred because it tolerates the coexistence of good and bad drivers on the road, a feature that does not apply to ordinary games. Road rules have a social function, which is to facilitate the achievement of the purposes of all persons who use the facility, regardless of what these purposes might be. And the rules are adjudged in accordance with their ability to satisfy this criterion.

In much the same way, the rules that constrain sociopolitical interactions—the economic and political relationships among persons—must be evaluated ultimately in terms of their capacity to promote the separate purposes of all persons in the polity. Do these rules permit individuals to pursue their private ends, in a context where securing these ends involves interdependence, in such a way that each person

	B's action	
	Follow adopted rule (drive left *or* right)	Adjust independently
A's action	Follow adopted rule (drive right *or* left)	I 10,10	II 5,11
	Adjust independently	III 11,5	IV −10,−10

Matrix 1.2

secures maximal attainment of his goals consistent with the equal liberty of others to do the same?

Concentration on the road rules example allows us to isolate another feature that is often overlooked. Rules provide to each actor *predictability* about the behavior of others. This predictability takes the form of information or informational boundaries about the actions of those involved in the interaction.

For example, suppose that in a small, developing country, automobiles are new and few in number. There has been both French and British influence in the country, so that early road users include both right-hand and left-hand drivers. As the number of automobiles increases, the absence of an established rule creates problems. Independent adjustment by each driver when two vehicles meet, with neither driver knowing how the other will react, produces a pattern of outcomes that is analogous to life in the Hobbesian jungle. All parties will be better off if they adopt a rule, *any* rule.

Matrix 1.2 illustrates this case. The game here is basically a coordination game, in that the rule adopted serves an informational purpose. Each of the two parties is given the ability to predict what the other will do. And it does not matter, by supposition, whether the rule adopted involves right-hand or left-hand driving, so long as the rule generates symmetric behavior. In such a case, there may be a role for government in announcing a rule. History, however, may do as well or better − for social conventions often serve to establish the relevant rules of conduct.

The interaction depicted in Matrix 1.2 differs from the more general dilemma game in Matrix 1.1 in the relative importance of the predictability content of the rule and the subsequent problem of enforcibility.

Matrix 1.2 depicts a game that is basically one of coordination; the major gains are secured on the adoption of a rule, *any* rule, and there is relatively little advantage to any player to be gained from defection. As shown in the matrix, however, there is *some* gain from defection and, hence, some enforcement problem. If A knows, for example, that B will always follow an agreed-on rule, then A will occasionally find it advantageous to depart individually from the adopted rule. But the temptation to violate the rule, once adopted, is not omnipresent as in the more general prisoners' dilemma setting.

A pure coordination game (not depicted in matrix form here) would be one in which the advantage of individual defection from adopted or conventional rules would be wholly absent, one for which there would be no enforcibility problem at all. Some such interactions surely exist. Language might be thought about in these terms. All persons in a social community have an incentive to use words that others understand. There is a natural force generating a common vocabulary and grammatical rules. The same description might be applied to the language of manners and etiquette whereby the apparent object of behavior is to convey meaning of some sort to others.

Other important characteristics of either the basic prisoners' dilemma interaction or the information–coordination interaction are obscured, however, in the Matrices 1.1 and 1.2. Both illustrations are directed toward the ultimate choice beween a rule and no rule. A second choice may involve a *choice between rules*, once the more inclusive game has been played, that is, once the need for a rule has been accepted by all parties. Consider, then, the case in which there is a difference between possible rules, even if we retain the assumption that there is symmetry in payoffs between the players. The "game" described here is really a "subgame" of that illustrated in Matrix 1.2.

Consider Matrix 1.3, which takes place "within" cell I of Matrix 1.2. The options of the two parties in this case are not those of adopting a rule and adjusting behavior without a rule. The choices are those confronted in the set of alternative rules. As depicted in Matrix 1.3, the rule "Drive right" dominates the rule "Drive left." It is important here to have a rule (shown in Matrix 1.2), but the question of which rule is also important. And because of the symmetry in payoffs between the players, both will, when given the constitutional choice, select the same rule.

Two points are worth making about the interaction depicted here. First, social conventions that emerge historically and take on the status of "unwritten rules" do not necessarily produce the best conceivable pattern of outcomes. Some modern social analysts (notably Hayek and

	B Choose "Drive right" rule	Choose "Drive left" rule
A Choose "Drive right" rule	10,10	—
Choose Drive left" rule	—	5,5

Matrix 1.3

his followers) display an apparent faith in the forces of social and cultural "evolution" to generate efficient rules. There seems to be no reason to predict that these forces will always ensure the selection of the best rules. In our example, the "Drive left" rule might well emerge and prevail − particularly if exogenous changes alter the relative payoffs to different rules over time. There may then be little or no evolutionary pressure toward the emergence of superior rules. This prospect alerts us to the need, periodically, to review alternative set of rules and to regard rules themselves as objects of choice, to be changed and re-designed according to the patterns of social states they generate. The prospect also alerts us to a possible role for "government" in the collectivity, that of facilitating a shift from old to new rules. "Govern-ment" in this context can be variously construed − as a consensually appointed assembly, the entire set of relevant players, or, at the other extreme, some random dictator-king. Since, in this example, the gains are symmetric, there are no particular advantages to being the rule chooser, but it may be important to have some person, group, or process that is empowered to choose among rules.

Second, the move from "Drive left" to "Drive right" *may not be desirable*, despite the dominance of the latter in the matrix. If rules are viewed as providing information to enable the players to predict each other's actions, it follows that any change in the rules *destroys* infor-mation. If the rule ("Drive right" or Drive left") is determined afresh each morning by the toss of a coin, there is no rule at all. In order to function, rules require stability. If rules are continually subject to change, the information they provide becomes negligible. Each player can no longer take it as given that others will abide by the rule in existence, even if he knows it himself, because he cannot know that others will know that he knows it. And when others may be playing by "outdated" rules, each has less incentive to play by new ones.

This argument suggests that there is a natural predilection toward conservatism in the constitutional perspective. The mere demonstration that state A would be "better" than the status quo, once state A were achieved, is not sufficient to demonstrate that a move from the status quo is justified. A "local" maximum may turn out to be a global maximum once the local maximum has been achieved.

Recognition of this fact reveals a crucial distinction between constitutional *design* and constitutional *reform*. In constitutional design, where there are no effective preexisting rules, all that is relevant is the choice between the rule that generates one set of outcomes and the rule that generates an alternative set. The rule that gives rise to the preferred set of outcomes is to be preferred. But when there is the question of changing an *existing* rule, as is the case in constitutional reform, the rule that generates the most preferred set of outcomes carte blanche is not necessarily dominant.

The argument here lends some force to the social evolutionist's antipathy to constructivist zeal. To the extent that stable and tolerable rules exist, a community may well be better off not to attempt change. Recognizing this claim does not, however, commit us to the view that the explicit reform of existing rules will *never* be desirable. The argument merely alerts us to the need for rules concerning the procedures by which existing rules might be changed, and in particular for ensuring that rule changes do not take place too often and without proper recognition of the transitional costs.

The basic coordination games depicted in Matrices 1.2 and 1.3 are simplistic in another important dimension. Quite apart from the ubiquitous conflict between individual and "social" interest, which creates the enforcibility problem, is the disagreement among individuals over the choice of rules themselves. This conflict potential has been deliberately suppressed in the coordination games discussed to this point. There is no difference between the two players in the ordinal ranking of the cells in the matrices.

Consider, however, a different example, still within the more general rules of the road category. For reasons already noted, it is clearly advantageous to have some rule; the setting is identical to that described in the "Drive right"–"Drive left" example. But suppose that there are two possible rules for behavior at intersections, only one of which can be chosen. One rule is "Give way to the right"; the other is "Give way to the left." Matrix 1.4 illustrates this interaction. Note that

B

	Select "Give way to the right" rule	Select "Give way to the left" rule
A Select "Give way to the right" rule	20,5	—
Select "Give way to the left" rule	—	5,20

Matrix 1.4

the ordinal ranking of the two relevant cells differs between A and B, with A much preferring the first rule, "Give way to the right," and B much preferring the second rule, "Give way to the left." Such divergent rankings may occur if, for example, A predicts that he will, on most mornings, approach an intersection from the right of B's approach.

The two players prefer different rules despite the fact that both prefer either rule to no rule. Because of the disagreement over which rule to adopt, however, there may be delay and dispute between the participants, each of whom will seek to maximize the distributional advantage promised by a choice among alternative rules.

The differential advantage placed on differing rules by different persons should not be overemphasized. To the extent that rules are long standing and that persons anticipate that they may occupy different positions in sequential plays of the game, the players may tend to reach agreement on the rule to be adopted much more quickly than the simple analysis implies. In our example, if the players predict that each will sometimes approach intersections from the right and sometimes from the left, the interaction can be modeled as in Matrix 1.2 rather than in Matrix 1.4.[4]

V.   Rules of the market order

Our purpose in Sections II and III was to isolate several elements of rules through the familiar examples of ordinary games, on the one

---

[4] For a general discussion of the principle that agreement on which rule to adopt is less difficult to achieve than agreement on strictly defined distributional allocations, see James M. Buchanan and Gordon Tullock, *The Calculus of Consent* (Ann Arbor: University of Michigan Press, 1962).

hand, and rules of the road, on the other. As noted, however, our central concern is with rules of economic—political order. In this section we shall introduce rules of the market, or economic, order and in Section VI we shall examine rules of political order.

In both of our earlier examples, the need for rules became apparent immediately upon reference to the interaction; one cannot conceptualize either ordinary games or traffic without thinking about rules. With respect to the far more important economic interaction among persons, however, the rules governing individual behavior within such interaction are often ignored. Economists, themselves, have been notoriously negligent in this respect. Complex analytic exercises on the workings of markets are often carried out without so much as passing reference to the rules within which individual behavior in those markets takes place. Adam Smith was not party to such neglect; he emphasized the importance of the "laws and institutions" of economic order.

The departure from this Smithian and classical emphasis is perhaps best illustrated in the "market failure" analytics of theoretical welfare economics, as developed in the middle decades of this century. "Markets" were alleged to fail when compared with the stylized, formal models derived from the economists' mathematical exercises. Analysis proceeded as if institutional constraints were totally irrelevant to the way in which individuals interacted within market structures.

The relevance of rules is perhaps best exemplified by reference to the familiar example of common-property resource utilization, sometimes referred to as the "tragedy of the common." If straightforward utility maximization is postulated to describe the behavior of users, the common will be predictably overgrazed. The market is alleged to "fail" in generating efficient usage of the scarce resource. As is by now familiar, however, the problem here is not with the workings of the market process, but with the rules within which the users operate. A change in the rules so that the scarce resource is separately and privately owned, along with means for enforcing and protecting individuals in rights of ownership, will remove the inefficiency. The example suggests that economists' proclivity to look at outcomes rather than at the rules that generate such outcomes has been a source of profound confusion. Reform of results or outcomes comes about through reform of the rules rather than through manipulation of the outcomes directly.

The normative thrust of the theoretical welfare economists was that of providing an argument for governmental or collective intervention in markets. A comparable pervasive oversight of the importance of rules characterizes the attitude of a group of economists who support market institutions in a normative sense. These economists have tended to neglect the importance of rules under the sometimes naïve presumption that the "market will out," regardless of institutional constraints. The presumption is that market solutions are sufficiently robust to swamp any institutional constraints that may exist. There seems to have been some confusion here between the robustness of economically motivated behavior within given constraints and the possible robustness of economically motivated behavior in modifying the constraints themselves. It seems quite possible that market outcomes may be robust within given institutions, while at the same time these institutions may be relatively insensitive to change without explicit and direct attention being brought to bear on their design and possible reform.

To return to a common-property example, there may be well-functioning markets in fish in which demand and supply forces operate to generate fully satisfactory allocative−distributive outcomes (given the resource and institutional parameters), while at the same time the absence of property rights in the fishing grounds fails to define a set of rules that are in any sense normatively ideal.

A second aspect of market rules deserves attention. In our earlier analysis of road rules, we found that the essential function of rules was to prevent individuals from inhibiting one another's actions: Rules had the essentially negative function of preventing disastrous harm. This is basically the task Hobbes assigned to the rules of social order that keep anarchy at bay. Within the Smithian vision of the market order, however, there is a significant *positive* aspect of human interaction. In Smith's view of the world, the division of labor mobilizes mutual gains from cooperation among traders, gains that each trader secures but that are beyond the capacity of any one person to comprehend fully. At each succeeding phase in the division of labor, each actor responds to his environment by exercising his creative imagination directly in his own interests and thereby indirectly in the interests of his fellows. The succession of such creative acts establishes an order that both reflects the enormous advantages of human cooperation and provides scope for additional creative acts to occur. At any point, one can contemplate the prevailing market order and recognize the nature and magnitude of the gains from human cooperation under the division of labor. But one cannot predict ex ante what the nature and magnitude of those gains will be. To do so would require the analyst to possess all the creative imagination currently spread over the entire set of economic agents.

Two things follow from this view. First, there is something necessarily nonteleological about the choice of market rules. How can the rules be chosen in the light of the particular outcomes to which those rules give rise if the precise nature of those outcomes is discovered only as they emerge? Second, when market institutions are inadequately defined, or some alternative rules apply that do not have the market's benign features, the true dimensions of normative "failure" cannot entirely be known. We can conjecture that the engine for harnessing human cooperation has not been fully operative — but what might have otherwise been necessarily remains a matter of speculation.

VI.   Rules of political order

Many social analysts might agree that market processes operate within reasonably clearly defined rules and that such rules are important objects of inquiry. They may be less willing to apply the same insight to political processes. But political "choices" also emerge from an interaction of individual agents within a set of institutional rules, with each actor being constrained by the actions of others. Political actors operate under a set of more or less clearly defined rules, and they make choices among the options available to them so as to maximize their returns (which may, here as in other settings, include ethical as well as economic objectives). The crucial issue is whether the set of rules that orders the relationships among the separate actors is that set which best leads individuals to further the interests of others, or at least refrain from imposing harm on others.

There are several ways of viewing political processes in the same terms as we view markets. The first, and most important at this point, is the view of political process as a system of interacting individuals from which outcomes emerge as equilibria. This view is consistent with any of a number of motives we might ascribe to those individuals and with any of a number of criteria by which we might evaluate the operative rules. The motives and criteria in question can be chosen from the economist's tool-kit. We shall explore such political applications of economic method in subsequent chapters. What is crucial here, however, is neither actor motive nor evaluative criteria but, rather, a prepardness to examine the political process in the same general terms as we examine markets. Individuals with their own objectives interact, under a set of rules (political institutions), to further those objectives, and the interaction finally serves to establish a particular outcome as an equilibrium. If the individuals' capacities and objectives are given, the only way the pattern of outcomes can be changed is by alteration of the rules. And changes in the rules, obversely, will alter the outcomes that emerge from any society of individuals.

Much of what we shall discuss in subsequent chapters concerns the implications of particular aspects of the political rule structure. At this point, we should alert the reader to the necessary subtlety of the rules–outcomes distinction in the political context. At one level, the rules of the political game are obvious enough: majority rule; periodic elections; various restrictions on the government's power to take; the requirement of systematic accounting for expenditure of public funds; the geographic structure of electoral arrangements, including possible partitioning of the political jurisdiction itself as under a federal structure; and so on. Yet many of these features themselves emerge from political process. Understandings, for example, of the appropriate domain of public activity, which have an important constitutional aura, are determined largely by ongoing political decisions. In this sense, the rules–outcomes distinction tends to become blurred in the political setting. Moreover, since both rules and decisions within rules themselves emerge from rather similar political processes, the significance of the distinction may seem somewhat overdrawn. It is precisely where the distinction is not obvious, however, that basic rules of the game may be at risk – and it is for this reason that we shall attempt to maintain the rules–outcomes distinction in the political setting.

VII.   The importance of rules

The first argument for the study of rules depends on the recognition of the role rules play in isolating an equilibrium outcome or pattern of outcomes for a community of social agents with given capacities and objectives. We have been at pains to point out that interaction among the same persons within any society may generate any number of social outcomes, depending on the rules that exist. But only those social outcomes are feasible that can be generated as equilibria under some institutional arrangement. For this reason, it is misleading to examine the set of all conceivable social outcomes and select as ideal what best fits some independent and external normative criteria. Institutional arrangements constrain the set of feasible outcomes no less significantly than the basic physical constraints ("endowments") that delimit the range of desired end products.

Lest we be charged with setting up a straw man here, consider the standard discussion of distributive justice, or "equity," in public-policy circles (a matter we shall take up in greater detail in Chapter 8). The standard procedure is to examine all distributions of total output that are consistent with the initial endowment of productive capacities and with the necessary loss in output involved in the redistributive process (although sometimes even the latter is ignored). On this basis, the set of conceptually feasible "distributions" is isolated, and some social welfare function or other piece of ethical apparatus is wheeled in to select the "best" from among them. But the natural constitutionalist question is, How are we to ensure that this "best" outcome emerges from political process? Surely it makes more sense to specify alternative sets of political rules and examine the distributions that emerge. If none happens to correspond to the "best" as earlier derived, then we must simply conclude that that "best" is not feasible.

The constitutionalist insists on the study of rules because he seeks to include all the relevant constraints within the analysis. To leave institutional constraints out of account is no less analytically reprehensible than to assume away limits on the productive capacities of economic agents or to ignore basic scarcity constraints.

The second argument for the study of rules is normative in nature, and it has several dimensions. We shall examine one of these in some detail in the next chapter, where we shall see that the choice among rules, because those rules will be operative over a long sequence of plays in which the fortunes of each player are somewhat uncertain, involves some special characteristics that are absent from the context of choice within rules where the positions of each player are well defined. Specifically, the natural predilection for conflict in the interests of players is substantially moderated in the choice over rules, extending the potential for agreement concerning rules among the players.

There is, however, another dimension to the normative argument for attention to rules rather than outcomes. This involves the claim that one cannot properly evaluate outcomes normatively unless one has information as to how the outcomes came about. Such a claim can be advanced on the ground that process is intrinsically of normative relevance or on the ground that information about process in turn provides information about the outcome without which evaluation is difficult or impossible.

Consider a simple example. Suppose that a particular economic outcome is advanced in which A has five apples and six oranges, whereas B has ten apples and nine oranges. The evaluation of that outcome depends in part on our acquiring information as to how it came about. Suppose that we discover it did so by virtue of A's simply taking six oranges that had previously been in B's possession. Presuming B's prior possession to have been evidence of legitimate title, the resultant outcome may be deemed normatively unattractive because it resulted from A's theft − because, in the process of bringing that outcome about, A violated normatively relevant rules of conduct.

In the same way, the outcome of some contest — a running race, for example — may not have any normative significance: Any outcome may be acceptable, provided the rules are fair and are adhered to. Alternatively, although outcomes *are* normatively relevant, so too may be the processes that generate them. An innocent man convicted erroneously of a crime might take some comfort in knowing that the trial was entirely fair, even though the jury erred as to fact. Similarly, a manifestly guilty man might find merit in the ritual of a totally proper trial, even though the outcome is a foregone conclusion. In both cases, the process as well as the outcome is relevant for normative purposes.

Rules may be normatively relevant in a different sense — not because processes according to certain rules are of independent value, but rather because adherence to certain rules provides information about the normative status of outcomes. This is particularly the case when the attribute of an outcome that is at stake is its efficiency. Specifically, if the allocation of apples and oranges between persons A and B results from free exchange between the two parties from some initial endowment point, and given that apples and oranges exhibit the properties of conventional "private" goods, we can presume that the resulting allocation is efficient, or at least that the trade satisfies the Pareto test. In the absence of information about how the final outcome had been reached, there would be no reason at all to presume efficiency. And, indeed, unless the analyst had the power to read the minds of the relevant individuals and discern thereby the utility function of each, it simply would not be possible to know. The fact that the outcome emerges from a process characterized by certain rules provides information about the normative status of the outcome that would not otherwise be available. Here, the normative significance is attached to the outcome, not the process, but the process nevertheless provides a test of the nature of the outcome.

CHAPTER 2

The contractarian vision

I. Introduction

Our purpose in this chapter is to describe the normative position from which we approach the whole set of issues involving the rules of social order. Through what window do we view the world of social interaction, actual or potential? Until we make ourselves clear in this respect, we may seem to be "speaking in tongues" to those whose perspective differs categorically from our own. Our position is explicitly and avowedly *contractarian*. This term alone will identify the conceptual framework to those familiar with classical political philosophy, especially with those works that embody the intellectual foundations of liberal society. To counter the most familiar and pervasive criticisms of this position, we must note that the contractarian construction itself is used retrospectively in a metaphorically legitimizing rather than historical sense. Prospectively, the model is used in both a metaphorically evaluative and an empirically corroborative sense.[1]

The relationship between the contractarian philosophical perspective and the rules-oriented, or constitutionalist, perspective is not so direct as it may at first appear. Section II examines this relationship and briefly discusses possible noncontractarian elements in constitutional thought. The contractarian perspective is grounded in individualistic presuppositions about the ultimate sources of value and of valuation. These precepts are examined in Section III, particularly in contrast to other, more familiar nonindividualistic teleologies. Section IV presents the contractarian paradigm in its most well-known setting, that of ordinary economic exchange. Section V extends the perspective to politics, generally considered. The unanimity requirement is examined in some detail in Section VI. And in Section VII the difference in the choice among rules and choice within rules is related to the unanimity requirement.

---

[1] For other attempts to describe the contractarian position, see James M. Buchanan and Gordon Tullock, *The Calculus of Consent* (Ann Arbor: University of Michigan Press, 1962); James M. Buchanan, *The Limits of Liberty* (University of Chicago Press, 1975); James M. Buchanan, *Freedom in Constitutional Contract* (College Station: Texas A & M University Press, 1977); and Geoffrey Brennan and James Buchanan, *The Power to Tax* (Cambridge University Press, 1980).

19

II.   Noncontractarian constitutionalism

As we emphasized in Chapter 1, the hallmark of the constitutionalist is the categorical distinction he makes between outcomes generated within defined rules and the rules themselves. Once this distinction is made, the effects of rules in constraining potential outcomes become obvious. Simple recognition of this linkage then prompts attention to the rules of social order as an object of inquiry and tends, almost necessarily, to generate an extended time dimension in all considerations of social policy or social change.

The constitutionalist, so defined, however, need not at the same time be contractarian. Understanding of, and respect for, the distinction between the rules that constrain behavior and the results of actions taken within the rules need not be derived from, or be the basis for, a contractarian position. Perhaps the most obvious example is the extreme conservative, the person who places value on existing rules because they do exist and have existed. Such a person may be constitutionalist in the full sense of the term; indeed, he may claim to be the only true constitutionalist since the ideal is a never-changing set of constraining rules.

A somewhat less extreme but closely related position is based on the recognition of the difference between rules as constraints and action within constraints but at the same time embodies the notion that the rules of social order are not artifactual creations subject to change. In this perspective, rules change slowly during the evolution of society. Although change takes place in the basic structure, it does so only through an organic evolutionary process. Hence, "reform" of the basic rules (of the constitution, broadly defined) is internally contradictory. The ordering function of social rules operates only because they are unchangeable in any directed sense.

A third position may retain apparent constitutionalist elements, but for reasons quite different from those that seem appropriate to the constractarian. A two-level structure of law may be envisaged, with the "higher law" embodying protection for a set of "natural rights" that people possess as human beings. In this interpretation, the "constitution" is that structure of institutions or rules that involves the protection of such natural rights, leaving to ordinary politics all other actions. And whereas the existing constitution may be modified, either in the direction of a closer correspondence with the desired protection of natural rights or in the direction of a further divergence from such idealized protection, there can be no change in the definition of the set of rights as such.

It is not our purpose to elaborate arguments that have been made in support of any one of the three positions sketched. Our intention is merely to indicate that each of the positions may have elements that seem constitutionalist in the common dialogues of the day. The contractarian rejects the first two positions because of the basically negativist implications they generate. If the rules of the socioeconomic−political game are not themselves artifacts subject to constructive change, there is little left to do but to endure the forces of history. The arguments advanced by both the status quo reactionary and the nonconstructive evolutionist are perhaps good counters to the romantic ramblings of those who speak naïvely about human perfectibility, but surely we must be given hope that the institutions of social order are subject to reform and change. If for no other reason, there would seem to be a moral obligation on the part of the social philosopher to provide such hope.

The differences between the contractarian and natural-rights theorists arise from quite other sources than do the differences between status quo reactionaries and evolutionists. The contractarian derives all value from individual participants in the community and rejects externally defined sources of value, including "natural rights." The discussion in Section II is as germane to the argument against the natural-rights position as it is to all other positions that derive value from external and nonindividualistic sources.

III.   Individuals as sources of value

The critical normative presupposition on which the whole contractarian construction stands or falls is the location of value exclusively in the individual human being. The individual is the unique unit of consciousness from which all evaluation begins. Note that this conception does not in any way reject the influence of community or society on the individual. The value structure of an isolated human being may be totally divergent from that of such a person described by membership in one or many social relationships. The presupposition requires only that societal or communitarian influences enter through modifications in the values that are potentially expressed by the individual and not externally.

If the individual is presupposed to be the only source of value, a question arises concerning identification. Which individuals are to be considered sources of value? There is no apparent means of discriminating among persons in the relevant community, and there would seem to be no logical reason to seek to establish such discrimination if it were possible. Consistency requires that all persons be treated as moral equivalents, as individuals equally capable of expressing evaluations among relevant options.

From these presuppositions, and these alone, it becomes possible to derive a contractarian "explanation" of collective order. Individuals will be led, by their own evaluation of alternative prospects, to establish by unanimous agreement a collectivity, or polity, charged with the performance of specific functions, including, first, the provision of the services of the protective or minimal state and, second, the possible provision of genuinely collective consumption services.[2]

As noted earlier, the empirical record of the establishment of historical states is essentially irrelevant to the contractarian explanatory argument. The fact that most historical states have emerged from conquest of the weak by the strong does not render unimportant or irrelevant the question, Can the existing state, as observed within the rules that describe its operations, be *legitimized* in the broadly defined contractarian vision? To deny the relevance of this question, and at the same time to hold to the contractarian presuppositions, would amount to making the charge that almost all observable states are illegitimate. In this case, the contractarian must join the ranks of the revolutionaries. If, however, within broad limits, the state can be legitimized "as if" it emerged contractually, the way is left open for constructive constitutional reform. Existing rules can be changed contractually even if they did not so emerge.

Note that in the conceptual derivation of the origins of the state just sketched, there is no resort to any source of value external to the expressed preferences of individuals who join together in political community. The state does not emerge to protect "natural rights." Nor does it reflect or represent the working out of some cosmic force, some will of God or gods. More important, the state does not exist as an organic entity independent of the individuals in the polity. The state does not act as such, and it cannot seek its own ends or objectives. "Social welfare" cannot be defined independently, since, as such, it cannot exist.

To this point, the contractarian defense has been relatively easy. A much subtler confusion arises when we raise questions concerning what it is that individuals seek to gain from political order, even when the basic contractarian presuppositions are granted. Even when the existence of nonindividualistic sources of value is denied, or apparently so, we are still left with individuals' own attitudes toward their

---

[2] This derivation is elaborated in some detail in Buchanan, *Limits of Liberty*.

activities as they enter into the idealized contractual dialogue. What do individuals seek when they attempt to reach an agreement with each other on rules governing their behavior and on rules limiting the exercise of state power in enforcing such rules? Do they seek "good"? Do they seek "truth"? Is collective organization viewed as a means or instrument of discovery, whether that to be discovered is described as "good," "true," or "beautiful"? Is politics analogous to science, or science to politics?

IV. Contract and exchange

Rather than plunge directly into the murky discourse suggested by such questions, we shall proceed circuitously by introducing a familiar setting. Ultimately, our interest lies with the participation of individuals in contractual agreement on changes in the most fundamental rules of the socioeconomic−political game in which they live. But a useful analogy is provided by ordinary market exchange, a contractual process in which we all engage and for which economists have well-developed analytic explanatory tools. We need only consider the simplest exchange model: a two-person, two-commodity trade or exchange.

First, let us think of two persons. A and B, each endowed with a bundle containing quantities of two goods or commodities, oranges and apples. For simplicity, let us assume that A initially has all the oranges and that B has all the apples. Both commodities are "goods" in the utility or preference functions of both potential traders, and there is not sufficient abundance in the endowments to satisfy fully the appetites of either person for either commodity. In this setting, trade can be beneficial to both parties. Person A will trade oranges for apples; B will occupy the reciprocal role. The two parties will agree to make exchanges so long as their internal trade-offs between the two commodities differ. When trading stops, at equilibrium, the internal rate of exchange between oranges and apples for A will be equal to that for B and will also be equal to the final terms under which the commodities were exchanged.

This is first-day economics, of course, but we seek here to look at this simple trading process from our contractarian−constitutionalist perspective. The implicitly postulated rules for trade involve the rights of each person to the initial endowments in his possession, along with the prohibitions on force and fraud in dealings. Within these rules, the two traders reached an outcome that can be described by a new endowment, a new imputation or allocation of the two goods between the two parties.

What can we say about the outcomes so attained? We can say that given the initial endowments and the existing rules of the trading game, the outcome is whatever *maximizes value*. But note that the source of value lies exclusively within the preferences of the persons who trade. There is no external source of evaluation, and trade as such is not merely a means by which some external, independently existing value is achieved. Individuals make their evaluations of the two commodities only as the trading process takes place, and, without trade, there could be no means of determining what value is at all.

Only through trading agreement can maximum value be attained. But note that this is not the same as saying that value is defined by agreement as such. In the process of reaching agreement, the traders are expressing values they place on the commodities. They are not deriving values from agreement; values are, instead, the elements that lead to agreement.

We deal with this matter in such detail here because there seems to be widespread confusion as to the connection between maximum value, or efficiency, and agreement. Professor Jules Coleman, in a well-informed critique of our position, has distinguished between what he calls epistemic and criterial usage of agreement in the definition of efficiency, or maximum value.[3] By epistemic usage of agreement, Coleman refers to the instrumental function of the contractual process. Hence, if there did exist some scale of value or valuation external to the traders, the trading process itself might be evaluated in terms of its success or failure in moving toward the maximum on such a value scale. In contrast with the epistemic use, Coleman introduces the criterial usage of agreement, by which he means that value is defined by the agreement per se. In the simple trading process analyzed earlier, we showed that neither of the two uses is involved. No scale of value exists external to the trading process. But in the expression of individual values through which agreement is ultimately reached, the traders are not deriving values from the end state of agreement as such. Their own, individually based values emerge as trade takes place; these values do not reflect feedback from the agreement itself.

The economist, who conceptually observes the trading process and who sees no violations of the basic rules, can assign an "efficient," or

---

[3] Jules Coleman, "Some Well Founded and Still Other Ill Founded Skepticism About Constitutionalism," in *Constitutional Economics: Containing the Economic Powers of Government*, ed. Richard McKenzie (Lexington Mass.: Lexington Books, 1984), pp. 141–55.

"maximum value," label to the equilibrium result. In so doing, he is not evaluating the result against any scale external to the participants in the trade, nor is he introducing some value scale of his own. Within the rules, as defined, the trading outcome must always be "efficient," and there is no way the economist can define an "efficient" allocation independently of trade itself. The economist is forced to bring his own evaluative criteria to bear on the rules of trade rather than on the results of trade.[4]

V.   Politics in the exchange perspective

We have discussed the simple trading example in some detail because the implications of the contractarian vision of politics can perhaps best be understood through the exchange analogy. In its most general terms, the contractarian paradigm for politics is the exchange paradigm, and analysis proceeds most readily in the familiar illustrations of trading in commodities. So long as the source of value is exclusively located in individuals and there is no differentiation among persons, the whole enterprise of politics can be viewed only as a complex many-person system of exchanges or contracts. Individuals must be conceived to join together to explore and ultimately to agree on the establishment of collective entities or arrangements that prove mutually beneficial.

"Trade" among persons in this setting will not, of course, take precisely the same form as the simple exchange of oranges and apples, both of which are privately partitionable and privately consumable goods. In politics, at the most general level, the result of "trade" among persons will be a set of agreed-on rules rather than a well-defined imputation of goods among separate individuals. At the simplest and most elementary level, that described by the initial leap from Hobbesian anarchy, individuals may reach an agreement to respect the property and person of individuals other than themselves. In such a trade, each participant secures the benefits of order, thereby reducing the need to expend his own resources in defense. In exchange, each participant gives up his own freedom of action in potential exploitation of the property and person of others, as defined in the contractual agreement.

This elementary conceptual example suggests that contractual agree-

---

[4] For an elaboration of the position outlined here, see James M. Buchanan, "Rights, Efficiency, and Exchange," in *Ansprüche, Eigentums- und Verfügungsrechte*, Arbeitstagung des Vereins für Socialpolitick, Basel, 1983 (Berlin: Duncker & Humblot, 1984), pp. 9–24.

ment on rules must precede any ordinary trading of partitionable goods. Unless there exists some mutually acceptable understanding of who has what rights to do what with what, when, and to whom, the more familiar marketlike exchanges cannot be initiated. To return to the earlier illustration, if persons A and B do not mutually acknowledge some property rights in oranges and apples as the initial endowments, they have no basis on which to begin exchange. Political order must, therefore, be antecedent to economic order, even if the exchange paradigm seems more natural when discussed in an economic than a political context.

The elementary conceptual–conjectural example also allows us to introduce several other principles that help clarify the continuing confusion in political–legal discourse. The rules of political order, including the definition of the rights of persons, can be legitimately derived only from the agreement among individuals as members of the polity. There is no basis for the commonly encountered notion that individual rights are somehow defined by governments. Individuals establish governments for the purpose of guaranteeing and protecting the rights agreed on in contract. Independent action by "government," or by persons who act as agents of government, to modify or to change individually held rights must violate the spirit of the contract. Of course, in the establishment of the political entity, powers of coercion are granted to governments, powers that are designed to prevent criminal trespass and exploitation of rights by internal and external aggressors. In the assignment of these powers, problems of control may arise, problems that are not amenable to easy solution. Once established as sovereign, government may not willingly remain within the limits of its initially delegated authority. To the extent that it exceeds these limits, however, government becomes illegitimate in its actions, even in the gloomiest of the Hobbesian visions of contract. Government may, in this setting, take on itself the role of redefining individual rights, but it does so in explicit violation of its contractually legitimate origins.

The non-Hobbesian vision of contract does not acknowledge that the sovereign must remain ultimately uncontrollable. The rules of political order may also lay down limits within which political units may take action, and, indeed, most explicit discussions of constitutional change involve questions of defining the limits of political rather than personal authority. The importance of making the basic distinction between rules and actions within rules emerges more forcefully in politics than in ordinary personal dealings. In private behavior, individuals are implicitly recognized to remain within their legally defined limits or rights. "The law," as an institutional structure, prohibits a person from invading the domain of others, or if a person does so invade, the law invokes punishment. Almost all of our ordinary behavior takes place within a well-defined structure of legal rules. In politics, however, the notion that collectivities, governments, also behave and should behave within the constraints of well-defined rules seems less "natural." The notion that constitutions define the limits of political authority is an abstraction that seems difficult for many to comprehend.

VI. Unanimity as the contractual ideal

Individuals are conceived as entering into discussion and ultimately reaching some initial agreement that both assigns separate individual rights and establishes an authority charged with the protection and enforcement of these rights. For this contractarian metaphor to be coherent, the agreement must be conceived to be inclusive. The terms must be accepted by all persons who are to be designated members of the group affected. Contractual agreement among a subset of persons, with terms to be imposed on others, would negate the legitimacy of the whole construction.

In an evaluative usage, an observed set of rules must be such as might conceptually have emerged from general agreement. The basic rules themselves, however, may well prescribe procedures for taking actions, privately or collectively, that do not require the consent or agreement of all members of the polity, either in actuality or evaluatively. Indeed, the distinction among levels of decision, exemplified in our fundamental two-stage emphasis on rules and behavior within rules, helps clarify this feature. There may be general agreement on a rule for taking political action (for example, determining the level of public outlay on education by a majority voting rule in a legislative assembly) that does not require approval by all members of the community. Or there may be unanimous agreement on a structure of legal rules within which persons in their private capacities may be allowed to take actions that other persons oppose (for example, entering into an established industry or profession).[5]

Even if, at a highly abstract philosophical level, the unanimity basis for establishing the legitimacy of the institutions of social order is acknowledged, on a practical level a requirement for unanimity may seem to be mere utopian romanticizing. Individuals come to the con-

---

[5] The discussion in this and the following sections is closely related to the analysis presented much earlier in Buchanan and Tullock, *Calculus of Consent*.

tractual process, even in its most idealized form, with separately generated values and with separately identifiable interests. The analogy with simple trade in partitionable private goods breaks down, or so it may be argued, because in any social or political contract, there must be agreement on the same rule, to be applied to all participants. In the exchange of apples for oranges, by contrast, agreement is facilitated by the simple fact that the two parties need not end up, after trade, with the same potential consumption bundle. If A and B, in the example, were somehow required to agree on a final allocation that assigned equal quantities of each good to each person, it seems likely that this requirement would preclude agreement altogether in many situations.

Quite apart from the "publicness" of any political agreement, however, is the even greater difficulty we confront when we consider the size of the trading group. With simple commodity exchange, or indeed any economic relationship, the agreement reached must ultimately include only two parties or agents in any directly participatory sense: one buyer and one seller for each good to be exchanged. The presence or absence of other buyers or sellers will, of course, affect the terms of trade between any two traders, but 2 remains the magic number for the economic analyst.

With political exchange, however, all parties must agree on terms. If we generalize from the simple economic exchange paradigm, any basis for expecting unanimous agreement on anything seems to disappear. In a situation where a unanimity rule is operative, each person is placed in a position, vis-à-vis all others, fully analogous to that held by a single party in a bilateral monopoly game. The incentives for strategic bargaining behavior seem maximal. At this point, however, the "publicness" of the result, noted before as restricting agreement in the economic exchange setting, partially offsets the incentives for strategic bargaining behavior. If the participants are constrained by the knowledge that any outcome reached must be equally applicable to all of them, they have much less incentive to try to hold out for purely distributional gains analogous to those promised to the successful strategist in the game of bilateral monopoly in goods.

VII.   Agreement on rules and the veils of ignorance and uncertainty

The seemingly convincing argument against the feasiblity of applying the unanimity criterion in imputing legitimacy to political rules is substantially mitigated if we recall once again the categorical difference between the choice among rules and the choice among alternatives within rules. For the latter, which we may call ordinary politics, elements of conflict seem to overwhelm elements of potential cooperation because the interests of individuals and groups are well defined and readily identified. The set of starting points, or possible positions of status quo, from which no change could ever be made under a unanimity rule would seem almost all-inclusive. In the economists' terminology, the Pareto-optimal set would be exceedingly large. This prospect is dramatically modified, however, when the choice alternatives are not those of ordinary politics but are, instead, rules or institutions within which patterns of outcomes are generated by various nonunanimous decision-making procedures. The scope for potential agreement on rules is necessarily wider than that for agreement on outcomes within specified rules.

This result follows directly from the fact that the interest of any person or group is much less easily identified in the choice among rules. It is much more difficult for a person to determine which of the several choice options confronted will, indeed, maximize whatever set of values that person desired to maximize. There are two reasons for this loss of interest identity as we shift to the level of choice among rules or institutions. In the first place, rules are, almost by definition, applicable to a number of instances or cases. That is to say, rules embody characteristics of "publicness" that need not be present in specific political outcomes. As an example, consider the position of a dairy farmer confronting choices at the two levels. He might strongly oppose a specific reduction in milk price supports, since such action will almost surely reduce his net wealth. At the same time, however, he might support a generalized rule that would eliminate political interference with any and all prices for services or goods. The effect of such a rule change or institutional reform on his own net wealth is less determinate in the latter case than in the former.

A related but somewhat different characteristic of rules is that they embody an extended time dimension. The very notion of a rule implies existence through a sequence of time periods. We could hardly describe a game by its rules if they were made up at the beginning of each round of play. Rules tend to be quasi-permanent; they "live" longer than outcomes of decisions made under them. A balanced-budget rule, for example, would be meaningless if it were adopted for only a single budgetary period. Such a restriction would be a "rule" in our sense only if it were known to remain in force for a succession of budgetary periods.

As both the generality and the permanence of rules are increased, the individual who faces choice alternatives becomes more uncertain about the effects of the alternatives on his own position. This relationship is perhaps most clearly illustrated when we postulate that individuals will try, generally, to maximize their expected net wealth. But this standard behavioral postulate of the economist's is not a necessary part of the analysis here. Regardless of what the participant seeks to maximize, the uncertainty about how particular rules will affect the value of his maximand increases as rules are made more general and more permanent.

The uncertainty introduced in any choice among rules or institutions serves the salutary function of making potential agreement more rather than less likely. Faced with genuine uncertainty about how his position will be affected by the operation of a particular rule, the individual is led by his self-interest calculus to concentrate on choice options that eliminate or minimize prospects for potentially disastrous results. Consider, for example, a political decision rule that would call for the random selection of one member of the community who would be authorized to make all decisions as to who would be put in prison and for how long. Even though each citizen, at the level of constitutional choice, would know that he had the same chance as any other citizen of being elected as the "dictator," this arrangement would almost surely be rejected. The potential losses from the exercise of arbitrary powers by the one person selected would far outweigh the expected gains. (Chapter 4 develops this point in more detail.)

To the extent that a person faced with constitutional choice remains uncertain as to what his position will be under separate choice options, he will tend to agree on arrangements that might be called "fair" in the sense that patterns of outcomes generated under such arrangements will be broadly acceptable, regardless of where the participant might be located in such outcomes. It was on the basis of this chain of reasoning that John Rawls introduced "justice as fairness." The affinity of the discussion here with Rawls's whole construction is apparent.[6] We have stressed uncertainty rather than ignorance, however, because the design of the choice alternatives themselves may influence the former.

The "veil of uncertainty" may be approached, if never fully realized, if persons are modeled as though they were faced with choices among rules of social order that are generally applicable and guaranteed to be quasi-permanent. By comparison, the Rawlsian "veil of ignorance" is an idealized normative construction, the appropriate starting point for persons when they consider making choices among basic principles of justice. Two objections have been raised to this construction. Can real

---

[6] John Rawls, *A Theory of Justice* (Cambridge; Mass.: Harvard University Press, 1971).

persons choose as if, behind such a veil of ignorance when, at another level of consciousness, they realize who they are? And does the construction have empirical bases in the commonly held feelings of justice? The partial veil of uncertainty, which we use and which was initially introduced in *The Calculus of Consent* (1962), is not subject to comparable criticism. It does not require persons who enter into the constitutional dialogues to shift moral gears. Persons are modeled as they are. The design of the choice alternatives must, however, affect their behavior, and in the limiting case, the veil is equivalent to that described much more fully by Rawls.

Another, and ultimately mistaken, objection that has been raised to the Rawlsian construction is not applicable to our own. In Rawls's formulation, the person in the original position behind the veil of ignorance knows nothing about his own prospective position under the chosen rules of social order – under the selected and potentially operative principles of justice. At the same time, however, the person allegedly knows everything about the general characteristics of the outcomes under such rules. This formalized construction has led several critics to charge that there is no contractarian element in the whole Rawlsian construction, contrary to what Rawls himself suggests, and that all such disembodied persons would automatically agree on the preferred option. This argument is mistaken on its own grounds because it neglects the subjective elements that must be present in predictions concerning the working properties of alternative institutions.[7] These subjective elements remain, of course, in the uncertainty representation of the calculus; these elements alone make contractual agreement necessary for validation. But, as noted, in the uncertainty representation, the two constructions attain full equivalence only in the limiting case.

VIII. Conclusions

Much of the discussion in this chapter has summarized material developed in earlier works within what may be called the contractarian strand of modern public-choice theory. We felt it necessary to include the material here in summary form, however, in order to maintain the potential interest of those who may not be familiar with the earlier contributions. Without some feel for the contractarian vision or para-

---

[7] For an elaboration of this point, see James M. Buchanan and Roger Faith, "Subjective Elements in Rawlsian Agreement on Distributional Rules," *Economic Inquiry* 18 (January 1980): 23–38.

digm from which we start and within which we work, the more narrowly focused, less familiar arguments advanced in succeeding chapters may seem to be free-floating irrelevancies.

One of our continuing frustrations has been the apparent unwillingness of our peers to acknowledge the importance of the several principles that, to us, seem elementary. The problem seems to be one of a difference in vision (paradigm, conception, or research program). In this chapter we have sketched our own vision; in Chapter 3 we shall try to describe and criticize the vision of the anticonstitutionalist.

The myth of benevolence

I.   Introduction

As we suggested earlier, the failure of the contractarian−constitution-alist argument to gain adherents in the broad community of scholar-ship in social science and social philosophy does not stem primarily from disagreement at the level of scientific analysis. Nor does it arise from basic ideological discord, in the proper meaning of this term, although the rhetoric of nonjoined debate often employs ideological charges to mask the absence of understanding. The problem is one of communication and understanding, at least in important part, rather than one of divergence in fundamental ethical norms. The anticon-stitutionalist does not know what we are talking about, quite literally, because he approaches the subject matter of social interaction from an alternative vision.

In Chapter 2, we tried to define and describe the contractarian vision or paradigm. But such a definition-description is not enough. We must also try to understand, as best we can, the opposing vision, the mind-set of the anticonstitutionalist, the foundations on which the same actual and potential world of social interaction is conceptualized. In the Nietzschean metaphor, we must try to look at the world through the *other* window in order to understand what it is that makes our own contractarian interpretation be so stubbornly rejected by so many of our peers. And we must do so as sympathetically as possible, forswear-ing the introduction of easy charges of analytic error or subversive intent.

We do not know much about the relationship between the accumula-tion of empirical evidence, broadly defined, and shifts in paradigms. We know that for almost all individuals, some such relationship exists, since people do change the way they view the world: Their perspec-

Precursory argument for some of the discussion in this chapter is contained in James M. Buchanan, "Politics and Science," *Ethics* 77 (July 1967): 303−10; reprinted in James M. Buchanan, *Freedom in Constitutional Contract* (College Station: Texas A & M University Press, 1977), pp. 64−80. More recent related discussion is contained in James M. Buchanan, "Sources of Opposition to Constitutional Reform," in *Constitutional Economics: Containing the Economic Powers of Government*, ed. Richard McKenzie (Lexington, Mass.: Lexington Books, 1984), pp. 21−34.

tives shift as they observe more and as they observe indirectly with the aid of science. We also know, however, that people shift their views of the world when they come to understand alternative interpretations of reality based on alternative visions, without the perceived empirical— historical record's having changed at all.

The difference between the contractarian—constitutionalist, on the one hand, and the anticonstitutionalist, on the other, does not lie in what each actually sees or observes. The difference lies, instead, in the way that each interprets what he observes or in the way that each fits his observations into an integrated structure of meaning. We want, in this chapter, to "explain" how the anticonstitutionalist looks at politics, the term "politics" here being most broadly defined to incorporate all aspects of social interaction. We can then compare and contrast this way of looking, this conceptualization, with that presented in Chapter 2. Since we are not ourselves proponents of the paradigm we seek to explain, our explanation must be treated as hypothesis rather than as an articulated statement comparable to that of Chapter 2.

We commence, in Section II, by plunging directly into the murky discourse circumvented only temporarily in Chapter 2 and promoted by the question of what individuals seek in politics. We must examine the meaning of "public good," as compared with "private good," which involves further discussion of the sources of value. Section III continues the discussion with a comparison between politics and science, both modeled as inherently social activities. Section IV is an attempt to demonstrate that the "truth judgment" paradigm leads almost inexorably to the myth of government benevolence. Section V explores the conceptualization of majoritarian democracy within this myth. Section VI then compares and contrasts the paradigm with our own in a more general philosophical setting.

II.   Private good and public good

What do people seek when they act in total independence? What do they seek when they participate in social interactions?

The first of these questions can be answered readily. People in isolated settings, Robinson Crusoe before the arrival of Friday, for example, seek what they want to seek: The question posed is relatively uninteresting. Economists might respond by saying that people seek "utility" and then proceed to model behavior in utility-maximizing terms. In this form, however, utility is operationally empty, since it becomes merely "what people maximize." Any number of comparable terms would be equally suitable: satisfaction, pleasure, happiness, or x.

The point is that for purely private choices made in isolation and outside any social relationship, individuals are presumed to establish their own private and internal value standards.

The second question is far more difficult. The economist who models individual behavior in idealized competitive settings only partially succeeds in escaping the social effects on individual values. In the abstracted model of the perfectly competitive economy, each participant remains totally unaware that he is involved in social interaction. Each buyer and each seller responds to prices that he confronts; his economic dealings remain wholly impersonal.

Economists recognize, of course, that the idealized construction is just that, and they acknowledge that even in the most competitive markets, descriptively identified, there may remain elements of a genuinely social relationship. Individuals, as buyers or as sellers, confront other persons on the reciprocal side of the market, persons whom they recognize as members of the human species. In such cases, the economic relationship is *social*.

At precisely this point, economic theory branches in two separate methodological directions. To the extent that a positive, predictive theory is sought, individuals who participate in economic exchanges continue to be modeled as if they do not recognize reciprocal trading parties as such. In order for operationally meaningful statements about choice behavior to be made, what individuals seek to maximize must be specified in advance. *Homo economicus* enters the scenario; individuals are postulated to seek only their own identified private interest, summarized in objectively measurable net wealth.

Quite another direction can be taken, however, if the economic theorist aims only at offering a logical explanation of the whole exchange network. In this approach, the person who recognizes the social nature of the exchange relationship may be allowed to incorporate the interests of the party on the other side of the potential exchange, and such incorporation may be allowed to modify choice behavior. In other terms, an objectively measurable maximand need not be specified. Nonetheless, even in this construction, the value to be maximized by the individual remains *internal* to his own psyche. This value may, as suggested, include some reckoning of the interests of the other party in exchange. But it is an interest subjectively experienced by the party other than the one on whom it is presumed to have an effect.

The point here is a subtle one, and it is a source of much confusion. Some detail may be warranted. Persons A and B engage in economic exchange; A recognizes the social nature of the relationship. Because he does so, he may not seek to maximize only his own net wealth. He may place some value on the well-being of person B, as he, A, evaluates this well-being. But such evaluation remains internal to A; it cannot be B's evaluation of B's well-being. The latter evaluation could not possibly influence the choice behavior of A.

This discussion of simple economic exchange is, again, useful largely because it aids in the analysis of the much more complex interaction of "politics." Initially, we may think of "politics" in an all-inclusive definition to refer to all interpersonal dealings other than the basic two-party, buyer−seller exchange that lies strictly in the domain of economics. As we indicated in Chapter 2, politics is modeled as "complex exchange" in the contractarian vision. But the motivation for individual behavior in such exchanges is necessarily more problematic than in simple economic exchange. In the latter, Wicksteed's methodological presumption of "nontuism"[1] allows the participants to be modeled as net wealth maximizers *in the exchange process itself*, while enabling the analyst to postulate any degree of altruistic behavior outside this process. The analyst of exchange concentrates on the in-exchange motivation and neglects beyond-exchange behavior, considering it to be outside the limits of his interest.

In "politics," however, no such presumption can readily be made. Consider a complex interaction in which *all* members of a politically organized community are potentially affected by the outcome of a decision that must be made between two courses of action. In other words, the setting is one in which "public good" or "public bad" is characteristic of the choice alternatives, "publicness" carrying the standard technical meaning here. If we now model the behavior of the individual as straightforward wealth maximization, we are postulating that the imputed interests of persons other than the individual examined are excluded. Clearly, this is a more extreme and hence less acceptable model of behavior than the comparable market exchange model. For this reason, social scientists, especially noneconomists but also many economists, have remained reluctant to work with net wealth maximization postulates for individual behavior in politics.

This reluctance is fully understandable, but a basic error is made when the postulate is dropped and analysis takes the alternative direction of allowing utility or preference functions to remain open. What do individuals seek in politics if they do not seek to maximize their own expected net wealth?

The idealists among us want to respond by postulating that participants seek "public good," that persons try, as best they can, to take the

[1] P. H. Wicksteed, *The Common Sense of Political Economy* (London: Macmillan, 1910).

interests of all members of the community into account when they
make in-politics decisions. The extent to which individuals are motivated in this way remains, of course, an empirical question. The point
to be emphasized, however, is that any degree of "other-regardingness"
can be incorporated, without difficulty, into the basic contractarian
paradigm. The contractarian, or complex exchange, model of politics
depends not at all on the postulated motivation of the individual actors.

The contractarian model does depend, however, on the presumption that the "public good" or "private good," or whatever mixture of
these might be relevant, is *internally conceived* and hence is *subjective* to
the person who acts. A person may, for example, behave strictly in
accordance with the idealist's norm; he may try to take into account the
interests of all others in the community. But such interests enter as
arguments in the choice calculus internally to the participant; the
interests of others are imputed to them as estimated by the participant.
These interests cannot reflect expressions of others in any direct manner.

The methodological–epistemological difference between the contractarian and the noncontractarian emerges at precisely this point.
When the noncontractarian postulates that the individual participant
in politics seeks "public good," what is sought is presumed to have an
external existence, outside the values and the evaluation activity of the
person who is expressing himself through his choice behavior. It is the
objective quality of what is sought that differentiates the noncontractarian from the contractarian position; it is not a postulated difference
in motivation.

If "public good" does exist in such an independently objectifiable
sense, it follows directly that the person who seeks this goal is deriving
his values from some source external to himself. Where such values
come from is never clear, and, or course, there may be many alleged
sources. We need not examine these here; we stress only that the
postulated existence of such objectively definable "public good" is not
consistent with what we have called the contractarian vision.[2]

---

[2] This is a jointly authored book, but any two authors must disagree on particular points
in a long and sustained chain of argument. In our case, we should acknowledge that
the argument in Section II, and related discussion in this chapter, is one such point.
The thrust of the argument is Buchanan's. Brennan, as well as some readers of the
manuscript in earlier drafts, has expressed misgivings about relating the contractarian
position so closely to the denial that objective values exist. It is suggested that there may
be an argument to the effect that objective values exist and that these include the value
of individual liberty. In the political context, this position might hold that contracta-
rianism requires only that individuals count equally in the ultimate origination of what
is to be expressed through politics. So stated, the position need have no implications
for the existence or nonexistence of objective value standards.

III.   Science, truth, and politics

We can clarify the discussion by making a distinction between two types of social interaction: between science and politics of the ordinary sort. This distinction is helpful because science is a social activity pursued by persons who acknowledge the existence of a nonindividualistic, mutually agreed-on value, namely *truth*, and who, furthermore, accept this value as the common goal of all participants in the enterprise. Science cannot, therefore, be modeled in the contractarian, or complex exchange, paradigm. Science is categorically different from the relationship that is the domain of economics. The contractarian contends that politics is best modeled as being analogous to the economic relationship; the noncontractarian contends that politics is best modeled as being analogous to scientific activity.

Science does, of course, make use of agreement, but it does so only in the epistemic sense noted in Chapter 2. Agreement among informed scientists is a test for the establishment of the truth of a proposition. But such agreement, in itself, does not ultimately validate the proposition. The validity as such remains conceptually independent of the belief of any scientist or of the commonality of belief among many or even all scientists. For this reason, any proposition is always subject to refutation, even if there exists unanimous agreement on its validity at a single point in time. The world was not flat in the Middle Ages because all "scientists" thought it was; nor is the world curved today because all scientists think it is. That which actually exists can never be known. But in the Middle Ages, the best available test supported the proposition of flatness, just as today the best available test supports the hypothesis of curvature. Our point is that in science, "what exists" is acknowledged to be wholly independent of the subjective judgment of any scientist or scientists.

In participating in the scientific enterprise, the individual scientist expresses a belief that certain propositions are "true." In so doing, he is not placing an individually derived value on the set of propositions as such. He is applying his own truth test or truth judgment. He is asking, "Is the proposition true?" He is not asking, "Is the proposition good for me?" or "Is the proposition good for society?" No value in a scientific proposition is akin to the value that the individual places on an economic result or outcome. It is appropriate for the participant in economic exchange to ask, "Is the extra orange good for me?" or "Is the extra orange good for the whole set of interacting traders?"

The question comes down to that of the place of politics in these two clearly contrasting paradigms. The anticontractarian−anticonstitutionalist's model of the social enterprise of politics is much like the model of science. Persons are seen to be engaged in a collectively organized, cooperative endeavor aimed at "discovering" some "public good" that is external to their own preferences or values. This "public good" exists, "out there," waiting to be found through the activity of politics. "Public good" is the holy grail. Finding it is fully analogous to finding truth in the scientific search process. By contrast, to the contractarian-constitutionalist it is inappropriate for the participant in politics to ask, "Is candidate A better than candidate B in promoting a 'public good' that is external to and common to us all?" Instead, the participant in politics should ask, "Is candidate A or candidate B best for me, in terms of my private interests?" or, perhaps more appropriately in a moral sense, "Is candidate A or candidate B best for the whole community membership, in my own assessment of that question?"

The jury as an example

The legal institution of the jury offers an example of the difference between the two conceptualizations of politics; it also allows us to construct a bridge between the discussion here and that of majoritarian democracy in Section V. The activity of the members of a jury is analogous to the activity of scientists. The jury is an institution charged with the task of establishing the truth or falsity of a proposition, and this truth or falsity is acknowledged to be totally independent of the subjective values of the jurors. The proposition that Mr. X is guilty of the crime with which he is charged admits one of two mutually exclusive judgments: Mr. X is guilty, or he is not guilty. But the finding of the jury does not in itself resolve the factual issue. Even if Mr. X is acquitted, he may remain factually guilty, and even if he is found guilty, he may be factually innocent. There is no direct relationship between the expression of the jurors and the fact of guilt or innocence.

The jury, as an institution, is an instrument designed to facilitate the discovery process. If it is efficient, as an institution, it may be the best available means of ascertaining judgments of guilt or innocence in situations in which one or the other of these verdicts is socially required. In its operation, the jury may use agreement among its members as a criterion for determining any collective judgment of the group. Individual members, like scientists, express their beliefs in the validity or invalidity of the proposition in question.

Because agreement is only a criterion that is instrumental to the institutional functioning, there is nothing intrinsic in agreement per se that dictates the appropriateness of the unanimity rule or, indeed, of any other decision rule. The best rule is the one that, on balance, seems to generate results that are in closest correspondence to the "truth," defined as that set of propositions that are ultimately nonrefuted. For the same reason, the jury itself, because it exists only as an institutional means of producing or discovering required judgments on the validity or invalidity of guilt–innocence propositions, may well be proved inefficient and replaced by alternative institutional forms. The random process of selecting jurors may, in particular, prove less efficient than some alternative that might rely only on "experts." Or as in many jurisdictional areas of law, a single judge may, as an "expert," be the most "efficient" vehicle for producing correspondence with independently desired results.

In the anticontractarian–anticonstitutionalist paradigm, politics is modeled as if the whole process were jurylike and concerned with finding or discovering "public good," just as the jury is concerned with determining guilt or innocence. Politics as a social activity is indeed like science. Values are external to the persons who participate, and agreement is only one of the instruments that may be employed to locate such values.[3]

IV.   The authoritarian imperative

The "politics as science" or "politics as truth judgment" conceptualization of the social interaction process is both authoritarian and antiindividualistic. These terms are intended to be descriptive rather than pejorative. The authoritarian imperative emerges directly from the extraindividual source of valuation of "public good." If "public good" exists independently of individuals' evaluations, any argument against the furtherance of such good because of some concern for individual liberty becomes contradictory. If "public good" exists separately from individuals' preferences, and if it is properly known, it must assume precedence over (although, of course, it could embody) precepts for maintenance of personal liberties.

The "politics as science" paradigm is antiindividualistic because it locates the ultimate source of value outside the psychological domain over which participants may express effective preferences. In a sense,

---

[3] Of course, none of this has any bearing on the question of whether a science of politics is possible or legitimate. A science of markets has developed that does not claim that market participants pursue anything akin to scientific truth. The science of biology does not necessarily invoke the assumption that organisms are "doing science."

the paradigm is "organic" or "organismic" in that it embodies a definition of "good" in application to the whole community of persons rather
than to individual members. In such a definition, however, there need
be no crude postulation of some organic unit — for example, "the
state" or "society." Individuals may still be reckoned to be the ultimate
units of consciousness; no supraindividual being need be hypothesized.
The "good" defined in application to the community remains, nonetheless, supraindividual because individuals cannot question its independent existence. Implicitly, all persons must agree that what is "good"
would be properly promoted if what is "good" could ever be found.

Once again the analogy with science is helpful. Michael Polanyi has
called the scientific community "a society of explorers." Implicit in this
conception is the presumption that individual scientists share the same
ultimate objective, truth, and that it is not legitimate for an individual
scientist to claim respect for his own beliefs merely *because they are his
own*. As it may actually be organized, the scientific community may or
may not appear to be working well in its avowed task of truth discovery.
It must nonetheless be conceived to be working within the limits of its
defined objective, the attainment of truth. For example, a hierarchically
organized laboratory may be deemed less efficient than a decentralized
laboratory, but scientists in the former are still modeled as behaving
within the limits of the overall objective. Because they are so modeled,
any overt limits or restrictions on their freedom of action must be
imagined as closing off possible directions of exploration. To impose
"constitutional constraints" on the activities of scientists, postulated to
be united in their search for truth, would seem itself authoritarian
rather than its opposite.

This analogy with science may suggest why anticontractarians view
with genuine fear and loathing modern proposals to impose constitutional limits on the exercise of political authority. In the mind-set
described, politics as an activity to be constrained makes no sense.
Those who advance proposals for such limits appear to be taking it
upon themselves to prejudge that for which the whole procedure is
established. Constitutional constraints on governments are like rules
that prevent scientists from entering certain territories for investigation. To the person who views politics from this perspective, there is
no logical basis for constitutional contract at all.

We have entitled this chapter "The Myth of Benevolence" because of
the implications of the paradigm. We can clarify these implications by
thinking of the social scientist or social philosopher who tries to
examine his raison d'être. In such an intellectual setting, the scholar
does not, and cannot, model his own behavior in any participatory

capacity, because he cannot acknowledge that his own values (or anyone else's) count. The activity of politics as such is carried out by
professional political leaders, whose behavior is described as that of
disinterested seekers after "public good" in the context of the various
issues that may be confronted. In this paradigm, these leaders are
neither agents for citizens, nor representatives of citizens' interests and
values. The scholar, on the sidelines, must almost by necessity model
his own behavior as that of a disinterested seeker one stage removed, in
a role as adviser or consultant to those who are more active participants.
The scholar is like the scientist in almost all respects, seeking "good" in
lieu of the scientist's "truth."

The scholar we describe here seems immune to the Wicksellian
charge that he proffers advice "as if" to a benevolent despot. He does so
because he does not understand the charge. Unless politics is modeled
in some version of the contractarian, or complex exchange, paradigm,
outcomes do not emerge from a process in which separate interests and
values are somehow amalgamated through a set of decision-making
institutions. Political outcomes are, instead, chosen by whomever seeks
the "good" in accordance with his own best judgment of what such
good is. There is no question as to the potential compromise or adjustment of separate interests. Those who disagree with the definition of
the "good" are misinformed and in error; they can be made to "see the
light" through the rhetoric of politics. In this setting, there is no way the
individual scholar can envisage a role for himself other than that of the
disinterested searcher for the "good," who has a claim to be better
informed than the ordinary citizen.

As he takes on the role as adviser to princes, whether imaginary or
real, the scientist-philosopher must oppose all suggestions for constitutional reform that involve additional limits on governmental authority,
and, for like reasons, he must support all proposals for relaxation of
existing constraints. Any overt restriction on political authority im-
pinges on the scholar's freedom of choice once removed. In the idealized search for political "good," the scholar-scientist needs to roam the
universe of potentially feasible space. The possibility set must remain
as open and inclusive as observed environmental parameters allow.

V.   Majoritarian democracy in the noncontractarian paradigm

We have suggested that the noncontractarian position sketched in this
chapter is authoritarian and antiindividualistic. We have not, to this
point, classified the position as nondemocratic, because vociferous

advocates of "democracy," particularly of its majoritarian variants, are among those who most strongly oppose constitutional change. The paradigm in which politics is analogous to science seems to allow the development of an argument supporting democratic institutions of collective decision making. Such institutions, perhaps best exemplified by majority voting rules in elected legislative assemblies, are defended, however, on grounds that are totally different from those that might be adduced from the contractarian paradigm.

The electoral machinery of democracy, considered as an institutional structure that generates collective outcomes, is conceptualized in a manner fully analogous to the conceptualization of a jury operating under unanimity or qualified majority voting rules. The machinery of democracy is supported because of its alleged efficacy in discovering "public good." Proponents of this position may, of course, acknowledge that democratic electoral processes, including plurality and majority voting rules, seem grossly imperfect when judged against some ideal standard. The plausible defense of democracy requires, however, only that these institutions be estimated to be less imperfect than suggested alternative arrangements.

In this context, majoritarian democracy may, indeed, find stout defenders, as the historical record surely suggests. Nonetheless, it should be evident that the intellectual foundations of democratic institutions in this noncontractarian perspective are weaker by an order of magnitude than those in the contractarian perspective. Democratic institutions stand or fall on their alleged superiority in generating the attainment of an independently existing "public good." The whole defense is necessarily based on *efficiency*. At a secondary level of argument, proponents of democracy in the noncontractarian paradigm acknowledge that majority rule is less imperfect than its alternatives in part because "public good" is not readily discernible. And, indeed, these very proponents may argue that nondemocratic methods of reaching collective decisions are more efficient when "public good" is more clearly outlined, as, for example, in war emergency.

By dramatic contrast with the defense of democracy in the noncontractarian perspective, the contractarian defense of democratic institutions, as constitutionally derived, is based on their ability to facilitate the expression of *individual values*. These institutions are not understood to be "discovering public good," even if at some deeper philosophical level the existence or nonexistence of such "public good" may be a subject of further inquiry. Since there is no external standard against which institutions can be evaluated in efficiency terms, any evaluative criteria must be applied directly to the institutional processes themselves. In such perspective, constitutional democracy, which may embody majoritarian voting rules in specified circumstances, is *categorically* distinct from all other governmental–political forms of authority. For the noncontractarian, on the other hand, there can be no categorical difference between, say, majoritarian democracy and hereditary monarchy. These are simply alternative forms of politics, both aimed at finding "public good"; the former is preferred to the latter only because it is more effective in achieving the purpose.

To the extent that a prejudgment has been made to the effect that majoritarian voting rules are more efficient in generating "public good" than are any of the alternative forms of political authority (for example, hereditary monarchy, aristocracy, oligarchy, rule by committee of a single party, or dictatorship by a military junta), any constitutional constraints on the "will of the majority" will tend to be opposed. Such opposition need not be based on any notion that the majority is always right; the notion is that the majority is more likely to be right than any other instrument for making collective judgments. To impose constitutional limits on the exercise of majority will must, therefore, imply that a majority in one period can claim superior wisdom to a majority in subsequent periods. Such a claim finds no reasonable basis for support in the noncontractarian framework of argument. Hence, majorities must be allowed to work their wills. The task of education remains one of informing political leaders and citizens about the content of "public good."

VI.   The aim of politics

We set out in this chapter to explain the noncontractarian–nonconstitutionalist vision of politics that stands in intellectual opposition to our own position, which we discussed in Chapter 2. In our attempts to do this, we frequently found it useful to introduce comparisons and contrasts with our own position. Our purpose in this section is to extend this comparison and contrast of the two paradigms to a more general setting. Central to the analysis will be the distinction between the application of evaluative criteria to end states or outcomes, on the one hand, and to processes or rules, on the other. The discussion will be related to the familiar distinctions made by philosophers between consequentialist and nonconsequentialist argument or, alternatively, between teleological and deontological arguments. As the discussion will demonstrate, it is relatively easy to classify the contractarian–constitutionalist position in terms of these categories; it is much more difficult to classify the noncontractarian position.

The contractarian–constitutionalist position is almost necessarily nonconsequentialist and deontological. Evaluative criteria must be applied to rules or processes rather than to end states or results, at least in any direct sense. As such, there is no means of evaluating any end state, because there is no external standard or scale through which end states can be "valued." End states must be evaluated only through the processes that generate them. What emerges from a process is what emerges and nothing more. If the process is such that individuals seem to be allowed to give due and unbiased expression to *their own values*, however these may be formed and influenced, the results must be deemed acceptable. (The particular posttrade allocation of apples and oranges between the two traders has *no* evaluative significance.) This process-oriented evaluation need not rule out possible feedback between outcomes and evaluations of processes. Patterns of outcomes generated under particular processes or rules may be such as to make the processes themselves unacceptable.

In this paradigm, however, politics as such has no aim or objective. Politics, broadly defined, is a complex institutional process through which persons express the values they place on the alternatives with which they are presented. It is internally contradictory to refer to "national goals," although, of course, individuals in a polity may share certain objectives.

As noted, it is much more difficult to place one of the familiar philosophical rubrics on the noncontractarian position outlined in this chapter. Again, however, the "politics as science" metaphor may be helpful. Politics in this paradigm is consequentialist and teleological in the same sense that science fits within these categories of argument. The activity as such remains nonconsequentialist and nonteleological because there is no predetermined objective that is known to participants and toward which all efforts within the activity are directed. Like science, politics is modeled as a discovery process, aimed at finding "public good." This end state, this good, is not known outside the activity of the search itself. But there is a critically important sense in which the whole argument is teleological. The activity of discovery, in science or in politics, is carried on under the continuing and pervasive presumption that what is sought exists independently of the expression of individual values in the search itself. Another way of putting this is to say that participants would agree that if the ultimate objective were known, all effort would be directed toward its achievement. Politics becomes a never ending search for the grail of "public good." This "good" is not to be defined by the values of the persons who conduct the search. Such persons seek something outside themselves.

CHAPTER 4

Modeling the individual for constitutional analysis

I.   Introduction

Any analysis of the effects of alternative rules on patterns of outcomes emergent from social interaction must embody some assumptions about the nature of the persons who interact. In this chapter, our objective is to set out our own assumptions and to defend them. This is no small order. The basic model of the individual that we shall advance as the most appropriate for comparative institutional or constitutional analysis − for investigating the implications of alternative sets of rules − is basically the *Homo economicus* construction of classical and neoclassical political economy. Earlier experience demonstrated to us that the use of this model, particularly outside conventional market settings, is widely regarded (even within the economics profession) as one of the most objectionable features of what has been called the new "economic imperialism." We do not propose to, and indeed cannot, restrict our discussion to behavior in alternative market orders. Much of our attention will be directed toward behavior in nonmarket institutions, and to behavior in political processes in particular. Hence, we shall have to confront the general antipathy to the use of the *Homo economicus* model in nonmarket settings and to deal with possible objections.

There is no question that such antipathy exists. In some of our recent work, for example, in which we attempted to develop a theory of the fiscal[1] and monetary[2] powers to be assigned to political agents, we modeled those agents precisely as their counterparts in market contexts are modeled by economists. The thrust of that work was to test the adequacy of constraints on the behavior of political agents under prevailing political institutions and to compare such constraints with those that might become operative under alternative structures. In part, we were examining the question as to whether constraints other than those present in the operation of electoral competition under

---

[1] See Geoffrey Brennan and James M. Buchanan, *The Power to Tax* (Cambridge University Press, 1980).

[2] See Geoffrey Brennan and James M. Buchanan, *Monopoly in Money and Inflation* (London: Institute of Economic Affairs, 1981).

majority rule might be required to secure tolerable outcomes for the citizenry.

Reactions to the work were predictably diverse, but there was no mistaking a widely shared skepticism about the use of the *Homo economicus* model for human behavior in political contexts. In one particularly strident commentary, for example, our "cynical" attitude toward human motivation was characterized as having "fascist"[3] over-tones. And in remarks to the American Academy of Arts and Sciences, no less a personage than Paul A. Samuelson advanced similar charges against "the boys from Chicago" and the whole tax limits movement.[4]

We therefore have both a personal and a professional interest in establishing the legitimacy of the *Homo economicus* postulate about human motivation, at least in the specific context of evaluating alternative social rules.[5] In more general terms, however, our experience is simply further evidence for the hypothesis that many social analysts feel most comfortable with some sort of "public interest" or "benevolent despot" model of government (or agents in governmental roles). Preference (often implicit) for the public-interest model may, however, stem not from empirical, intellectual, or ideological foundations but from sheer analytic convenience. The public-interest model enables the analyst to proceed with normative policy evaluation unhindered by any concern with policy implementation. To judge a social outcome "unsatisfactory" by some ethical standard is, almost definitionally, to reckon that that outcome ought to be changed. The manner in which such a change is to be secured is not a matter to be taken too seriously at the purely ethical level, but the implication seems to be that since the problem is a "social" one, "society" must act. And since the notion of society "acting" is strictly meaningless, it seems natural to replace society with its agent, the "government." In this mind-set, the implicit presumption that government will, in fact, do what is normatively suggested may not appear to be relevant. The implications of "social ethics" as distinct from "private ethics" seem to be that government either has or ought to have the powers to act as the analyst recommends

---

[3] See John Foster's summary review of our *Monopoly in Money and Inflation* in *Economic Journal* 91 (December 1981): 1105.

[4] See Paul A. Samuelson, "The World Economy at Century's End," *Bulletin of the American Academy of Arts and Sciences* 34 (May 1981): 44.

[5] Two of our papers, "The Normative Purpose of Economic Science," *International Review of Law and Economics* 1 (December 1981), 155–66 and "Predictive Power and the Choice among Regimes," *Economic Journal* 83 (March 1983): 89–105, represent earlier efforts to justify the use of the *Homo economicus* construction in constitutional analysis.

and that the government will so act once the moral force of the normative recommendation is understood. Of course, the analyst might respond by saying that no such implications are intended in his exercise. He might conceive his task to be limited to the specification of what policy options are "good" and what options are "bad"; the implicit model of government and politics becomes a mere methodological convenience for him. He would defend his procedures by arguing that the evaluation of policy options is a useful exercise, quite apart from any attempt to model political behavior explicitly. So it may be; but as we have previously noted, a similar argument could be made in support of exercises involving the imagination of undiscovered realms of resource and energy potential. We suggest that even if advanced solely for convenience in evaluating what the analyst thinks are relevant policy options, the benevolent despot model of politics and government has promoted and sustained monumental confusion in social science, and social philosophy more generally.

We do not propose to introduce the *Homo economicus* model for any comparable analytic convenience. Nor do we wish merely to strike some sort of balance between this model, on the one extreme, and the benevolent despot model, on the other. Our use of *Homo economicus* stems from our conviction that this model is the most appropriate one for constitutional analysis. The remaining sections of this chapter deal with various lines of defense of the *Homo economicus* construction in the constitutional context.

II.   *Homo economicus* in politics: the argument for symmetry

On the basis of elementary methodological principle it would seem that the *same* model of human behavior should be applied across different institutions or different sets of rules. The initial burden of proof must surely rest with anyone who proposes to introduce differing behavioral assumptions in different institutional settings. If, for example, different models of human behavior were used in economic (market) and political contexts, there would be no way of isolating the effects of changing the institutions from the effects of changing the behavioral assumptions. Hence, to insist that the basic behavioral model remain invariant over institutions is to do no more than apply the ceteris paribus device in focusing on the question at issue.

If an individual in a market setting is to be presumed to exercise any power he possesses (within the limits of market rules) so as to maximize his net wealth, then an individual in a corresponding political setting must also be presumed to exercise any power he possesses (within the limits of political rules) in precisely the same way. If political agents do not exercise discretionary power in a manner analogous to market agents, then this result must follow because the rules of the political game constrain the exercise of power in ways the rules of the market do not, which is to say that the constraints are not comparable in the two settings. Otherwise, there must be an error in analysis or observation. No other conclusion is logically possible, given the invariance of the behavioral model across institutions.

This procedure does not, of course, rule out the possibility that actual behavior in differing institutional contexts will be different. What it does exclude is the introduction of behavioral difference as an analytic assumption. If behavioral differences are attributable to differences in rules, it must be possible to link the rules in some way to the behavioral patterns they generate, without resort to separate fundamental models of behavior, which can do nothing but guarantee emptiness in any attempted institutional comparison.

We propose to analyze behavior as economists generally do, that is, in terms of the choices among alternative courses of action faced by individual agents. The conceptual apparatus here involves a radical separation between means and ends − between opportunity sets and preferences. "Explanations" of outcomes are advanced with reference to the relative prices or costs of the options (and of changes in those prices) rather than to the preferences of the agents. In this sense, for the economist, the only differences in institutions that are relevant for explaining behavioral differences are the differences in the prices of the alternatives. Pure differences in preferences (that is, differences that cannot ultimately be traced to differences in relative prices) wrought by institutional change cannot be brought within the explanatory power of the economist.[6]

The analytic approach that relates preference shifts to institutional differences skirts dangerously close to, and may be indistinguishable from, the use of models wholly different from those mentioned earlier. Such an approach might suggest that individuals assume roles that are institution-dependent, that in politics, for example, persons take on character roles as "statesmen," whereas in the market they take on character roles as "possessive profit seekers." In ignoring this whole approach and the literature in which it has been developed, we realize

---

[6] For an ingenious attempt to bring what appear to be our preference shifts into the relative-price explanatory framework, see George Stigler and Gary Becker, "De Gustibus Non Est Disputandum," *American Economic Review* 67 (March 1977): 76–90.

that we are limiting our realm of discourse and dialogue. But the analytic presumptions in support of behavioral symmetry at the most basic level seem so strong that the onus of proof must lie with those who would advance the institution-dependent behavioral model.

The symmetry argument may seem elementary and self-evident, but its acceptance surely carries us part of the way toward the use of *Homo economicus* in politics, at least among those economists who remain content to adhere to such a behavioral model in their analyses of markets. In a more general sense, of course, the symmetry argument does nothing to establish *Homo economicus* as the appropriate model of human behavior. Alternative models may be introduced. The symmetry argument suggests only that whatever model of behavior is used, that model should be applied across all institutions. The argument insists that it is illegitimate to restrict *Homo economicus* to the domain of market behavior while employing widely different models of behavior in nonmarket settings, without any coherent *explanation* of how such a behavioral shift comes about.

III.   Science and the empiricist defense

The use of the *Homo economicus* model requires more specific support. The most natural, and perhaps most familiar, argument is that people do, in fact, behave as the model suggests, at least on average and in the large. Due allowance must, of course, be made for the degree of abstraction necessary to introduce any generalized model and hence for instances of specific violation of the behavioral postulate. But once such allowance is made, the argument is that *Homo economicus* offers a better basic model for explaining human behavior than any comparable alternative. Most modern economists would probably take this position, which receives its most explicit defense from members of the modern Chicago school.[7]

The position is difficult to reject, and for two reasons. First, if one insists on a comparison of *Homo economicus* with alternative behavioral models of roughly equal levels of abstraction and generality, many of the grounds for debate are swept away. Models of behavior that are psychologically richer may be rejected because of their failure to meet the implicit austerity test. Second, and more important, *Homo economicus* is not well defined, and the would-be critic may find that his quarry has disappeared, only to reemerge in another guise. In specify-

---

[7] See, for example, George Stigler, *The Economist as Preacher* (delivered as the Tanner Lectures, Harvard University, 1980).

ing *Homo economicus* as a net wealth maximizer, for example, one may fail to explain much of what can be observed, but the observations may not be definitive because the defender of the model may resort to changes in the specification of the choosers' utility functions. In other words, the defender of *Homo economicus* deflects the criticism of the content of preferences by the claim that the structure of preferences rather than content is the central element of the model.

As we shall indicate in Sections IV and V, our defense of the *Homo economicus* model is basically methodological rather than empirical. Nonetheless, the methodological defense requires empirical presuppositions, and we can be quite specific in this respect. We simply require that demand curves slope downward, which, in turn, requires that it be possible to identify the "goods" individuals value. That is to say, our empirical presuppositions refer to the signed arguments in individuals' utility functions and do not involve trade-offs among these arguments. Furthermore, we require that individuals consider their own interests, whatever these may be, to be different from those of others.

For economists whose purpose is quite different from our own, who seek to provide a positive-predictive "science of behavior," whether in market or political settings, further specification of the model is required. And as research results have indicated, *Homo economicus*, as an all-purpose explanatory model, runs into some apparent difficulties. Analysts are hard put to explain such behavior as individual voting in large-number electorates, individual volunteers in defense of the collectivity, and voluntary payment of income taxes. Fortunately, for our purposes, we are not required to discuss possible tests of the usefulness of the *Homo economicus* model in this all-inclusive explanatory sense.

The reason is that for our constitutional argument, it is sufficient to defend the *Homo economicus* construction as a "useful fiction," while largely setting to one side the question as to just how "fictional" the individual in the model may be. Indeed, we make the stronger argument that *Homo economicus* is uniquely useful for purposes of comparative institutional analysis and for ultimate constitutional design. But as previously noted, the argument here is methodological and analytic rather than empirical.

IV. A methodological defense of the differential interest model of behavior

A central presupposition in our methodological framework, then, is that individuals have interests that conflict. We can show how this presupposition is relevant to our constitutional analysis by introducing a simple analogy.

Suppose that A is thinking of engaging another person, B, to do something that A wishes to be done and that requires a substantial advance payment; for example, B may contract to build a house for A. Any defection on B's part from his contractual obligation will impose costs on A, costs that may be significant. Hence, A will seek to limit the scope of such possible defection and will do so even if A thinks the likelihood of B's defection is low. In the example, A will first inquire about the reputation of alternative builders before engaging B and, presumably, would not contract with B at all if the prospects for defection seemed high.

Despite this threshold acceptability of B, once agreement is reached A may hire a lawyer to draw up a formal contract. And for purposes of the contract itself, A will make the working hypothesis that B is a rogue who is out to defraud him if the opportunity permits. He makes this hypothesis because this is the contingency the formal contract is designed to cover. In other words, the nature of the contract-drawing exercise leads A to make assumptions about B's motivations that A may well believe to be a poor reflection of the empirical realities.

Nothing here is said about whether drawing up the formal contract is or is not justified. This decision will depend on the relative costs of the exercise. What the argument does suggest is that if the formal contract is to be executed, the ascription of differentially self-interested (*Homo economicus*) motivations to the relevant party or parties is a logical part of the operation. The reason for the contract as such is its possible function in modifying B's private interests in such fashion as to make these interests congruent with A's. The focus in such a precautionary exercise is necessarily on B's differential and separable interests.

Note that we do not need to claim that private interest, as it is normally defined, is the only or even the predominant motivation for human action in order to justify such a focus. Once we acknowledge that private and differentially identifiable interest is relevant at all to human behavior, a comparison of alternative institutions must attend primarily to the question of how those institutions operate when individuals act in pursuit of their separately defined interests. If there were no conflict among interacting agents, that is, if interests were not differentially identifiable, then, of course, there would be no concern about how alternative sets of rules might modify and transform such conflicts. But to deny that there are conflicting interests among persons is to engage in an absurd flight of fancy. Individuals' objectives differ. Conflict exists, and the investigation of alternative institutions is ultimately motivated by some criteria of conflict resolution. In all such meaningful investigation, we simply must assume that agents' interests conflict in order to focus on the central purpose of the whole analysis. In so doing, we are merely adjusting our analytic microscope to focus it on the subject of our concern.

When we examine the properties of the idealized market order, for example, we can agree with Adam Smith that the consumer does not depend for his supper's meat on the benevolence of the butcher, without in the least ruling out the existence of such benevolence. The butcher may or may not be benevolent toward his customers. The crucial point is that such benevolence *need* not be present, and hence whether or not it is present is essentially irrelevant. Speaking more generally, if we want to examine the extent to which a particular set of rules, such as that of the market order, succeeds in transforming the self-oriented interests of human agents into actions that further the interests of others, it is but natural for us to assume that such agents are entirely self-oriented, even if, empirically, they may not be. If we want to discover how institutional rules can turn conflict into cooperation, we cannot simply assume that persons who operate within those rules are naturally cooperative. Such a procedure would amount to removing the whole problem by assumption.

In any evaluation of alternative institutions, therefore, *Homo economicus* is a uniquely appropriate caricature of human behavior, not because it is empirically valid but because it is analytically germane. Where the question of empirical validity arises is in evaluating the importance of the whole contractual or constitutional exercise. An institutional setting that operates so as to transform private self-interest into behavior that is profitable to individuals other than the actors, and that does so more effectively than other institutions, is relatively more valuable to the extent that private self-interest does motivate human behavior. If individuals tend naturally to be other-regarding in all but a few minor aspects of their behavior, then a preference for institutions that channel self-interest toward furtherance of the general interest is less pronounced, and other possible criteria for institutional evaluation become relatively more important. At base, therefore, empirical issues determine the significance of the whole constitutional exercise. But the analytic method for constitutional analysis is a separate issue, and in our dealing with the question of analytic method, empirical considerations do not enter, save in the threshold manner already indicated.

V.   Social evaluation and quasi−risk aversion

We shall proceed with a somewhat varied elaboration of the theme introduced in Section IV. We have perhaps not yet fully established the case for the use of *Homo economicus* in the generation of normative conclusions about the choice among alternative sets of rules. In particular, we have not discussed the implications of the elementary fact that more restrictive rules will not only help to prevent the occurrence of disaster but also often preclude actions that may be intended to promote desirable outcomes.

Consider an issue that was widely discussed in the early 1980s: the proposed "balanced-budget amendment" to the United States Constitution. We can analyze the role of constraints within existing political institutions[8] by means of the self-interest behavioral model for actors. We can make some predictions as to the effects of the existing constraints of electoral competition on the proclivity of political agents, or coalitions, to create budget deficits. We can then ask how the behavior of these agents might be modified by the introduction of an enforcible balanced-budget constraint. But any complete analysis would also have to reckon with the possibility that such a balanced-budget rule, if operative, might sometimes restrict well-intentioned and far-seeing politicians from securing macroeconomic stability. (We do not propose to enter into the debate concerning whether systematic governmental intrusion in the macroeconomy can, even in theory, exert a stabilizing influence.) In one perspective on politics at least, any implied reduction in the governmental flexibility of response to unforeseen circumstances will embody potential costs that must be taken into account.

It is obvious that the degree of disinterested and far-seeing behavior on the part of political agents will be relevant to the comparison of expected costs and benefits of alternative fiscal rules. The model of self-interest, or *Homo economicus*, will tip the balance of argument in favor of assigning less discretionary power to political agents than would be the case under the benevolence model. In this sense, the *Homo economicus* model is not innocent, and its claim to empirical relevance must be addressed.

Even at this level of inquiry, however, the mere empirical record can be very misleading, particularly if this record is interpreted in a strictly predictive manner. That is to say, if we seek a model of human behav-

---

[8] We have made several efforts to do so. See, particularly, James M. Buchanan and Richard E. Wagner, *Democracy in Deficit* (New York: Academic Press, 1977); and Brennan and Buchanan, *Power to Tax*.

ior that corresponds to some "best" prediction, either in the technical sense that the variance from observed values is minimized or in the heuristic sense that some fair average of observed behavior seems to fit, and then, at the second stage, try to compare institutions on the basis of such "best fit" models, the results will be systematically biased in the direction of inadequate constraints. For these reasons, the *Homo economicus* model may be justified despite the fact that it embodies more cynicism about persons' behavior patterns than the simple evidence warrants. To put the same point differently, if we array models of behavior along a conceptual spectrum from "worst case" to "best case" poles, the model that is appropriate for making a comparison among social arrangements is somewhat closer to the worst-case pole than that corresponding to the simple "average" description of behavior.

The line of reasoning here is that there is, in the evaluation of institutional alternatives, an intrinsic feature that imposes a sort of risk aversion on the evaluator. We should emphasize that we do not assume that individual citizens, either behind some veil of ignorance or as located in society, are inherently risk-averse in the normal meaning of this term. For our argument here, we may take individuals to be strictly risk neutral. It is the peculiar setting of choice that causes the individual to behave *as if* he were risk-averse – hence, our use of the phrase "quasi–risk aversion" in the title of this section.

Our claim is that because of the nature of what is to be evaluated, the gains attached to an "improvement" secured by departures of behavior from the modeled are less than the losses imposed by corresponding departures of behavior in the opposing direction, that is, toward behavior worse than that represented in the model itself. To express the argument in terms of the worst-case, best-case spectrum, as we move from the best-case pole to the worst-case pole, predicted social losses (costs) increase at an accelerating rate. The harm inflicted on his fellows by a person who behaves "worse" than the average person in the community is greater than the benefits provided by another person who behaves "better" than the average person. Accordingly, the average-person model understates the average harm done. In imagining scenarios that might emerge under various sets of rules (a process that is essential before a choice is made), citizens will act as if they were risk-averse. There will be a rational "bias" toward avoidance of the worst-case prospects.

Nothing more is required to sustain this claim than the elementary apparatus of economic analysis. We need only assume, first, that sets of rules are instrumentally valued in the sense that they are expected to facilitate the provision of what can be conceptualized as valued goods and services. From this assumption it follows that these goods and services can be quantified, in terms of more or less. Second, we assume that goods and services are not costless; the polity-economy operates within an overall scarcity constraint. Finally, we assume that the demand curves for these goods and services slope downward.

1. The monopoly example

We shall elaborate the argument by means of an extended example, the results of which can then be generalized to institutional comparisons of all types. The example involves a comparison of competition and monopoly. Elementary theorems in welfare economics demonstrate that efficient resource usage occurs when there is complete freedom of entry given specified technical conditions that must be satisfied. In the equilibrium of such an industry, there are no unexploited gains from trade. Implicitly, this model of competition assumes that all persons are net wealth maximizers. By extending the same behavioral assumption to (nondiscriminating) monopoly organization of the same industry, the analysis demonstrates that efficient resource usage does not characterize the equilibrium results. There will be welfare losses, in comparison with the ideal outcome, that stem from restriction on entry: There are unexploited gains from trade.

The magnitude of these welfare losses will depend, however, on the assumptions made about the monopolist's behavior. In the textbook models, monopolists are modeled as net wealth maximizers, but other possibilities are no less plausible a priori. For any number of reasons, the monopolist may refrain from charging the profit-maximizing price – to discourage entry by other firms, out of sheer inertia, or to further the perceived "public interest."

If the purpose were to develop a theory of monopoly behavior that would be of assistance in predicting the pricing and the output strategies of firms that are in monopoly positions, appeal to the empirical record would seem entirely appropriate. From such a record, we might be able to derive a maximand for the simple monopolist that would yield the best prediction of price–output behavior, a maximand that would embody both private-interest and public-interest arguments, as empirically relevant. Our point is that such a predictive model is *not*, in general, appropriate for the estimation of welfare losses from monopoly organization.

For the sake of simplicity, assume that all monopolists fall in two groups. One-half of all monopolists are strict profit maximizers in the pure textbook sense; the other half are pure "public interest" firms,

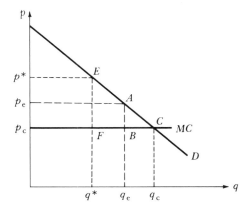

Figure 4.1

and these set prices and outputs at the level attained in full competition. In this setting (and assuming linear demand curves), the best single model is one in which price is set halfway between the profit maximizing price, say, p^*, and the competitive price, say, p_c. If the good is provided under monopoly conditions, in many separate locations, and the demand curve in each location is that labeled D in Figure 4.1, then the best single prediction of price in any location will be $p_e = 1/2(p^* + p_c)$, with the corresponding output q_e.

If this best-fit model of monopoly behavior is now used to estimate the welfare losses of monopoly organization in general, we should proceed to estimate welfare loss for each location in the amount ABC in Figure 4.1, with total welfare loss being this quantity summed over the n locations. This total would then purport to measure the excess value that all persons (consumers and monopolists) would be prepared to pay (in terms of the value of other goods forgone) to secure a guarantee of the efficient outcome.

Such analysis would, however, simply be wrong. The area ABC does not provide the best measure of the per-location welfare loss of the monopoly form of organization. The expected per-location loss attributable to monopoly is one-half of the loss under the profit-maximizing model plus one-half of the loss under the public-interest model of behavior (the latter is zero by assumption here). In other words, the expected welfare loss per location is one-half of the area CEF (Figure 4.1), which is larger than the area ABC.

If we measure welfare loss as a function of output over the relevant range, we obtain Figure 4.2. The W curve shows the relation between

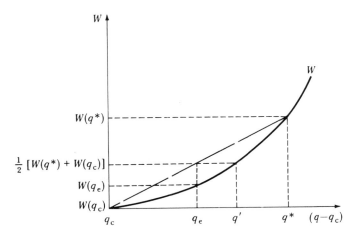

Figure 4.2

welfare loss and output and is based on the measurement of the triangles subtended in Figure 4.1. We use the more or less conventional formula[9] $W = (\frac{1}{2}dp/dq)(q - q_c)^2$. The central point is that W is a "convex function" of the difference between actual and ideal output. This means that the welfare loss at the best-fit output level q_e, which is $W(q_e)$ in Figure 4.2, is characteristically less than the best-fit welfare loss, which is $\frac{1}{2}[W(q^*) + <W(q_c)]$. That is, the expected cost of monopoly is greater than the cost associated with expected monopoly behavior, because the profit maximizers do proportionately more harm.

There is, of course, a single model of monopoly behavior that will yield an appropriate estimate of the costs of monopoly – namely, the model that generates q' in Figure 4.2 as the average monopoly output choice. Our basic point here is that *this* model of monopoly behavior is *systematically more cynical* (that is, closer to the worst-case end of the spectrum) than simple empirical inspection of monopoly behavior would suggest. Consequently, something reasonably close to the simple textbook model of the profit-maximizing monopoly may be justified, even though at least some monopolists behave in a way more congruent with "public interest" provided that the objective of the model is to lay a basis for the normative evaluation of alternative institutional forms.

[9] See Arnold Harberger, "Three Basic Postulates for Applied Welfare Economics," *Journal of Economic Literature* 9 (September 1971): 785–97.

2. The general case

The central point is much more general than the monopoly example. Models of behavior used in social analysis are often evaluated simply by appeal to the "facts." It seems clear that to many analysts these "facts," distilled from simple observation, from introspection about themselves in policy roles, or more elaborately from consultation of the historical record, suggest that those who hold discretionary power under a particular institutional regime will often be constrained by internal moral considerations from acting in a self-interested way. Suppose that this is so. Nevertheless, any model of behavior derived from a simple "average" of observed behavioral patterns will not be sufficient for comparative institutional analysis. An appropriate behavioral model will have to reckon with the fact that the harm inflicted by those who behave "worse" than the notional average will be proportionately greater than the "good" done by those who behave "better" than the average. Accordingly, a bias toward the worst-case end of the behavioral spectrum is entirely justified. Specifically, *Homo economicus* can be used as a model for comparative institutional analysis even when the empirical record (however described) indicates that its allowance for the relevance of public-interest motivations is inadequate.

We have presupposed that political and market institutions are valued not in themselves but for their potential capacity to allow the generation of desired goods and services. If this analytical framework is accepted, it seems natural to conceptualize individuals at the constitutional level as making determinants over possible institutional arrangements in a manner analogous to the choice between monopolistic and competitive market forms. Using the *Homo economicus* behavior model in constitutional analysis, and justifying this use on analytic rather than empirical grounds, is a procedure we have borrowed from the classical political economist-philosophers in their analysis of political institutions. And we can, perhaps, do no better in this connection than appeal to David Hume: "In constraining any system of government and fixing the several checks and controls of the constitution, every man ought to be supposed a knave and to have no other end, in all his actions, than private interest."[10]

---

[10] David Hume, "Of the Independency of Parliament," *Essays, Moral, Political and Literary*, Vol. 1 (London: Oxford University Press, 1963).

VI.   Gresham's law in politics

Our final argument in defense of the *Homo economicus* model is at least as old as Thomas Hobbes. It embodies the notion that when many persons are involved in a social interaction, the narrow pursuit of self-interest by a subset will induce all persons to behave similarly, simply in order to protect themselves against members of the subset. As Hobbes stated, "Though the wicked were fewer in number than the righteous, yet because we cannot distinguish them, there is a necessity of suspecting, heeding, anticipating, subjugating, self-defending, ever incident to the most honest and fair-conditioned."[11]

Hobbes might well be interpreted here as presenting a version of the risk-aversion argument similar to that elaborated in the previous section. But he might also be interpreted claiming that there is what we would call a sort of Gresham's law in social interactions such that bad behavior drives out good and that all persons will be led themselves by the presence of even a few self-seekers to adopt self-interested behavior.[12]

One way of constructing the relevant analytics would be to follow the obverse of Gary Becker's theory of social altruism.[13] In Becker's theory, if an agent, A, acts benevolently toward a person, B, and B then has the opportunity to undertake some activity (at small cost) that will in turn benefit A, then B can be induced to take such action out of self-interest. For example, suppose A gives B one-quarter of each dollar that A receives at the margin. Suppose, furthermore, that B can, at the cost of one dollar, undertake some act that secures a benefit to A worth more than four dollars (or equally prevents a harm to A worth more than four dollars). Then B will rationally undertake that act and secure the benefit for A: A's initial altruism toward B stimulates a reciprocal altruism on the part of B, despite the fact that B does not really care about A at all. For the more inclusive social group, the argument suggests that a critical mass of altruists may tend to create an apparently altruistic society, one in which some share of mutual gains is exploited through reciprocal nonexchange behavior.

Suppose that in such a society, the number of altruists declines or that the directly reciprocal relationships required for Becker's model

---

[11] Thomas Hobbes, *De Cive* (1642) (New York: Appleton-Century-Crofts, 1949), p. 12.

[12] See, for example, J. Roland Pennock, *Democratic Political Theory* (Princeton, N. J.: Princeton University Press, 1979), pp. 521–4.

[13] Gary Becker, "Altruism, Egoism and Genetic Fitness," *Journal of Economic Literature* 14 (September 1976): 817–26.

to work become blurred and ambiguous. The incentives for nonaltruists to behave altruistically may then dissipate rapidly; the structure of expected reciprocation unravels. The rational person, facing choice at the constitutional level, may seek to select institutions that depend only minimally on altrusitic behavior as a protection against any erosion of reciprocation that might be present.

The Hobbes argument could, therefore, be made consistent with the Beckerian vision of social interaction. But a more direct, though related, interpretation may be more relevant. We might think of a situation directly contrary to that analyzed by Becker, one in which some person, say M, enjoys the imposition of harm on another, N. Suppose that it costs M one dollar to impose a dollar's worth of harm on N and that M spends one-fifth of his income indulging in this sort of malice. Suppose, furthermore, that N does not care about M, one way or the other. Nonetheless, if N can act so as to reduce M's income by one dollar, he has saved himself twenty cents worth of harm. Hence, N will be led to act to damage M, despite his total disinterest. That is to say, M's malice is contagious. Moreover, if, as Hobbes suggests, the M's in the community are ex ante undetectable, the N's may be led to act in part maliciously toward everyone on the chance that anyone encountered may be an M, at least to the extent that such behavior is not excessively costly.

Consider a more plausible situation in which some persons in the community are mildly altruistic and some are truly selfish. Suppose that individuals are linked together through some interactions that are prisoners' dilemma settings of the sort depicted in Matrix 4.1. (The construction of a matrix of this type was discussed in Chapter 1.) In this case, the numbers in the cells of the matrix represent money returns (in dollars) to the players. If each player acts so as to maximize his own money payoff, the socially disastrous outcome emerges.

The distinguishing feature of the game depicted in Matrix 4.1 is that the gain to each player from the selection of strategy 2 is much smaller when the other player selects strategy 1 than when the other player selects strategy 2. Note that the incremental gain to A from playing a_2 is only one dollar if B plays b_1, but the gain to A from playing a_2 is twenty dollars if B plays b_2. Suppose, now, that A is indeed mildly altruistic and derives some value from B's receipt of payoffs, say ten cents on the dollar. This altruism is not sufficient to induce A to make direct transfers to B, since such transfers would cost A one dollar for each dollar receipt for B. But A may well refrain from inflicting harm on B to secure a gain for himself, provided that the "terms of trade" are within certain limits. If we depict the payoffs to A in Matrix 4.1 in terms

A's choice	B's choice	
	b_1	b_2
a_1	[4,4]	[−20,5]
a_2	[5,−20]	[0,0]

Matrix 4.1

A's choice	B's choice	
	b_1	b_2
a_1	[4.4,	[−19.5,
a_2	[3,	[0,

Matrix 4.2

of their utility equivalents, rather than as money payoffs, then under the assumption of the mild altruism postulated, we get Matrix 4.2. Note that in this setting, there is no dominant strategy for A. His preferred strategy now depends on what B is predicted to do. If A knows that B is symmetrically altruistic, A will then play a_1 confident that B will respond by playing b_1. If, on the other hand, A knows that B is a narrow maximizer of self-interest, then A also will be induced to play as a narrow maximizer. In this game, A's mild altruism becomes behaviorally relevant only if A believes B to be mildly altruistic; otherwise, the socially disastrous outcome emerges as before.

We shall return to the Hobbesian citation and postulate that A does not really know whether or not B is a maximizer. In this case, A would need to have an expectation that among the various B's he encounters in the prisoners' dilemma setting, 90 percent would behave symmetrically in order to induce A to play a_1. There is a threshold number of "righteous" altruists below which all will behave as if purely selfish, simply to protect themselves against the prospect of playing against a narrow dollar maximizer. Consequently, even if the "virtuous" are more numerous than the "wicked," all may be induced to behave "nonvirtuously," with predicted consequences.

This result is reinforced if we model social interactions in many-person terms. If each person finds himself in prisoners' dilemma settings in which many other persons are involved — in which there are many B's and not just one, as in the simple matrix illustration — then predictions must be made about the behavior of all other persons in the interaction. For example, suppose that A faces ten B's in a setting like that shown. Most of the B's can be predicted to behave reciprocally in response to altruistic action by A, but so long as one person in the B group does not, the gains from this mode of behavior on the part of A may well be dissipated.

An additional element emerges, particularly in the many-person interaction, that may prevent voluntary altruism from exerting much behavioral influence on social outcomes. Consider the setting just discussed, in which a single person, A, faces ten B's. Suppose that A continues to act altruistically, within limits, despite his prediction that at least one B will try to exploit the situation and to secure differential gains. The remaining B's, initially, will respond symmetrically to A's gestures of goodwill. But as these B's observe the single defector to be securing differentially high gains, their inherent sense of unfairness may induce them to act nonreciprocally toward A. The attribute of fairness summarized in the phrase "getting my share" may be an important motivation that prevents the spread of other-regarding behavior.

In summary, the spirit of Hobbes's analysis is that although altruistic and public-spirited motivations may be widespread among the population, these are delicate flowers, and crucial to their blooming may be the existence of institutions that do not make social order critically dependent on their effectiveness. To this extent, the implications of the Hobbesian argument are that institutions should be designed with *Homo economicus* in mind, and that altruism, like good manners, can be appreciated but not "presumed upon."[14]

---

[14] The Hobbesian argument seems to be the same as that implicit in the admonition of D. H. Robertson when he advised all economists to issue warning barks when they saw proposals depending on "love" for their effectiveness. See D. H. Robertson, *Economic Commentaries* (London: Staples Press, 1956).

There is, finally, a quite different, non-Hobbesian sense in which something like Gresham's law may apply in social interactions. Lord Acton's famous dictum that power corrupts, and absolute power corrupts absolutely was, no doubt, based on some predicted psychological destruction of the moral fiber of the despot. Such considerations are beyond our purview in this book, but there is a related, if quite different, point to be made. If institutions are such as to permit a selected number of persons to exercise discretionary powers over others, what sort of persons should be predicted to occupy these positions?

In yet another market analogy, suppose that a monopoly right is to be auctioned; whom will we predict to be the highest bidder? Surely we can presume that the person who intends to exploit the monopoly power most fully, the one for whom the expected profit is highest, will be among the highest bidders for the franchise. In the same way, positions of political power will tend to attract those persons who place higher values on the possession of such power. These persons will tend to be the highest bidders in the allocation of political offices. Economists have only recently become interested in the welfare properties of the political bidding process, under the rubric of "rent seeking."[15] In the rent-seeking literature, the focus of attention has been on the net resource wastage involved. Here we voice a different concern. Is there any presumption that political rent seeking will ultimately allocate offices to the "best" persons? Is there not the overwhelming presumption that offices will be secured by those who value power most highly and who seek to use such power of discretion in the furtherance of their personal projects, be these moral or otherwise? Genuine public-interest motivations may exist and may even be widespread, but are these motivations sufficiently passionate to stimulate people to fight for political office, to compete with those whose passions include the desire to wield power over others? If procedures are such that power *is* allocated to those who value it most highly, then there is some presumption that those who might want the values of *all* to weigh in political decisions will be driven out. Since the demand for discretionary power is highest for those individuals who desire social outcomes different from outcomes that perhaps most others would choose, political institutions will be populated by individuals whose interests will conflict with those of ordinary citizens. Citizens will need to plan for their institutional life accordingly.

---

[15] For a collection of the relevant papers, see James Buchanan, Robert Tollison, and Gordon Tullock (eds.), *Toward a Theory of the Rent-Seeking Society* (College Station: Texas A & M University Press, 1981).

VII. Summary

Homo economicus, the rational, self-oriented maximizer of contemporary economic theory, is, we believe, the appropriate model of human behavior for use in evaluating the workings of different institutional orders. The central feature of the *Homo economicus* model in this connection is its presumption of the ubiquity of conflict among interacting agents; it is this presumption that underlies the skepticism toward the possession of power that characterizes our attitude (and that of classical political economists) toward the design of institutions. Such skepticism means that it cannot be presumed that discretionary power possessed by agents under a particular institutional regime will be exercised in others' interests, unless there are constraints embedded in the institutional structure which ensure that effect. In this sense, our model lies a great distance from the predominant "benevolent despot" model of politics in which public-interest orientations are assumed simply as a matter of course.

In mounting our defense of the *Homo economicus* alternative, we have focused on analytic and methodological arguments rather than purely empirical ones. Our arguments are several:

1. There is a strong analytic case for undertaking the comparison of institutions with the *same* basic behavioral model, rather than shifting behavioral horses midstream.
2. To the extent that institutional design is supposed to transform private-interest motivations into public-interest behavior, it makes analytic sense to focus on private-interest motivations and abstract from any purely behavioral altruism.
3. If market and political institutions are valued instrumentally for their capacity to produce goods and services that citizens want, and if the preferences for these goods and services exhibit standard convexity properties, it is rational for citizens to design institutions assuming a model of political agents' behavior that generates "worse" outcomes than the empirical record would suggest emerge on the average.
4. Unless there is a critical mass of altruistically inclined individuals, which might be a substantial majority of citizens, it may well pay even the altruistically inclined to behave selfishly.
5. Because those who bid most for power in institutional orders will tend to be those whose private projects require major modification in the behavior of others, all citizens can rationally expect discretionary power to be exercised in ways that will be uncongenial to themselves.

There is, of course, empirical content in these arguments. However, in contrast with the purely predictive "science of behavior" models of conventional economics, empirical aspects are not entirely decisive. The significance of this fact is not that we believe that the purely empirical case for the use of *Homo economicus* is weak, although we believe that case to be rather weaker than some of our more zealous colleagues do. The significance is rather that the empirical record is singularly difficult to unravel, not least because observed behavioral patterns may be substantially influenced by the prevailing institutional structure, so that when that structure is altered there are entirely predictable but (necessarily) currently unobservable behavioral changes. Consequently, rather than attend to ultimately inadequate observations, we have attempted to develop our argument on the basis of reasoned speculation. Of necessity, such reasoned speculation makes up a large part of constitutional analysis. And as for our political-economist forebears, so for us: The *Homo economicus* – derived model of social conflict and cooperation seems uniquely appropriate for our constitutional speculations.

CHAPTER 5

Time, temptation, and the constrained future

Preface

Preceding chapters have offered a philosophical—methodological perspective from which an emphasis on the rules or institutions within which social interaction takes place more or less naturally emerges. In this chapter, we offer *reasons* for rules in a more specific sense. Any binding rule is, of course, a constraint on behavior. Hence the question, Why should a person, or persons, deliberately choose to impose constraints on his or their own freedom of action?

There are several answers to this question, the applicability of each depending on the choice setting with which one is dealing. Our initial emphasis in this chapter is on the *temporal dimensionality* of individual choice, on the effects that recognition of this dimensionality exerts on choice behavior itself, and notably on the choice of rules. That is to say, we examine the implications of the simple fact that people choose among alternatives in the knowledge that their choices will affect the options available to them in subsequent periods. These effects are important and worthy of analysis regardless of the choice setting. But as noted, and as the discussion will suggest, the effects differ among settings, notably between individual behavior in private- and collective-choice roles.

Recognition of the temporal dimensionality of choice provides one "reason for rules" — rules that will impose binding constraints on choice options after the rules themselves have been established. That is to say, in either a private-choice or a public-choice role, persons may choose to restrict their own futures, and such behavior may be wholly rational.

The chapter is divided into two parts: The first analyzes individual choice in a private setting; the second analyzes individual choice in a collective-decision setting.

Preliminary treatments of the material contained in this chapter can be found in two papers by James M. Buchanan: "History, Now, and the Constrained Future" (presented at the Interlaken Seminar on Analysis and Ideology, Interlaken, Mich., May 1982), and "Individual Choice Behavior in Private, Agency, and Collective Decision Roles" (presented at the Club Turati Conference on Individual and Collective Rationality, Turin, Italy, January 1983).

PART 1: INDIVIDUAL PRIVATE CHOICE

I.   Introduction

The commonplace warning that "we start from here" prefaces any serious discussion of institutional–constitutional change. In a casual treatment, the "here" is atemporal. Our emphasis is instead on the temporal element. Not only must we start from here, defined as where we are, but we must also start *now*, in the present. We cannot undo events that have already taken place. We may, of course, reinterpret our history, but we cannot go back in time and reverse its course.

We can act only now; we cannot act in the past. But neither can we act in the future. We confront choice options now, not later, and although the action that we take now may influence the choice of options available to us later, along with our possible orderings of these options, the fact remains that we cannot, in the present, make choices in future time. Nonetheless, the choices that we make now must embody the recognition that we will also face choices at some later date.

II.   The ultimate Z's

We shall relate the analysis here to modern developments in the theory of individual choice behavior, notably to the work of Gary Becker and his colleagues.[1] In that work, the arguments in an individual's utility function have been redefined so that they represent composite "commodities," the Z's, which are themselves produced by the household through combinations of inputs, the X's, which are purchased as ordinary goods in the marketplace. Household production functions describe the relevant trade-offs among the separate inputs, the X's, that are variously combined to generate the Z's. The individual is modeled as maximizing utility, defined over the Z's, given the market or shadow prices for the X's, within some overall income constraint.

From this basic construction, it is relatively straightforward to shift one stage back in the individual's decision process and to drop the income constraints by including leisure, or desired usage of time, as a Z commodity with its own shadow price. We can then model the individual as choosing a whole profile of behavior, constrained by time, talent, and initial endowments. This one step back in the decision sequence would seem to be as far as most modern economists could go. They

---

[1] See Gary Becker, *The Economic Approach to Human Behavior* (University of Chicago Press, 1976).

would not seek to go farther back in the imagined choice chain, to get behind the set of composite commodities, the Beckerian Z's. Economists become uncomfortable when they are unable to specify arguments in utility functions.

Our interest here, however, is not in further elaboration of the analysis of utility maximization in the orthodox economists' framework. Our interest lies, instead, in moving beyond the Beckerian Z's to what we might call the "ultimate Z's." Our concern is with an individual's selection of a life-style, or behavior pattern, in a more comprehensive setting than any that might be conceptualized as the maximization of a function defined over a set of known arguments. The individual may choose a life plan, a sequence of actions, that he hopes will ensure that his experiences are "interesting," "good," "rewarding," and/or "happy."

There must, of course, be minimal attainment of the Beckerian Z's for the achievement of such experiences. The basic human needs — food, clothing, shelter, sex, security, liberty — will place bounds on feasible life-styles. But, essentially, individuals in modern Western society have long since attained levels of affluence that enable them to transcend these elementary biological determinants of behavior.

III.   Preferences for preferences

To what extent are the preferred trade-offs among the ultimate Z's chosen? Can we really go much beyond the Beckerian Z's? Can we say anything about the formation of preferences? Can we discuss meta-preferences meaningfully?

More can be said once we recognize that individuals make choices sequentially over discrete time periods and that choices made in one period influence those made in later periods. We stress here that we seek to do more than introduce the capital investment aspects of current-period choices. We can readily incorporate such aspects into the standard framework by defining a relevant Z as "consumption in time t_i," hence allowing a person at time t_0 to devote available resources to the production of that Z. This analysis implicitly presumes that the individual chooses only at t_0. No multiperiod choice is introduced, although the temporal interdependence of utility is embodied in the analysis.

We propose to examine genuine multiperiod choice in a setting where the individual, having chosen among the relevant Z's, all dated as of time t_0, moves through time to find himself at t_1. He is not the same person who confronted choice at t_0, and this fact will be taken into account when the initial choice is made at t_0. At t_1, the individual will be a "product" of choices that have been previously made at t_0 and over the whole sequence of periods t_{-1}, t_{-2},..., t_{-n}. Within relevant limits, the individual constructs himself as an acting and choosing entity by the actions taken in periods before that in which choice is now confronted.[2]

The individual has a private, personal *history*, and this history will have shaped both the preferences and the constraints that interact to determine choice behavior in any period t_0. A person who has never tasted wine cannot exhibit a preference for "good" wines even when the standard constraints allow such options to be within the potential consumption bundle. A person who has not trained for long-distance running cannot compete in the Boston marathon regardless of a strong desire to do so.[3] In the conceptualization here, an individual is analogous to a specific capital good, a machine designed and constructed with a determinate form and shape and, therefore, capable of being used over a relatively limited range of functions, departures from which can be made only at some anticipated costs in efficiency.

Rationality precepts require that this temporal interdependence be recognized. A rational person, temporally located at t_0 and given a personal history, will recognize that current-period choices among relevant Z's will, in turn, directly affect the range of Z's that will be potentially attainable in t_1 and beyond and, also, that current-period choices can shape, to an extent, the Z's that will be preferred in later periods. "The individual" at t_1 will be predicted to be some continuity of the person who faces the choice options at t_0, the individual "constructs" the chooser at t_1 and beyond, as well as the set of choice options, within limits. (The limits of the interdependencies are not important for the analysis as such.) A preference ordering of the set of possible "persons at t_1" that the chooser reckons to be feasibly attainable would seem no different, conceptually, from a preference ordering of a set of basic Z commodities.

---

[2] This self-construction aspect of choice has been discussed in some detail by James M. Buchanan, "Natural and Artifactual Man," in *What Should Economists Do?* ed. James M. Buchanan (Indianapolis, Ind.: Liberty Press, 1979), pp. 93–112.

[3] For purposes of our analysis, it is not important to distinguish between shifts in constraints and shifts in preferences. Stigler and Becker argue that it is helpful to treat all such shifts as changes in constraints, under the postulate that preferences remain uniform both over time and among persons. In either case, the individual who chooses does so in the knowledge that his choice behavior at one time can affect his potential choice actions at other times. See George Stigler and Gary Becker, "De Gustibus Non Est Disputandum," *American Economic Review* 67 (March 1977): 76–90.

If such a preference ordering is admitted to be possible, and if current-period choices are acknowledged to affect the choices to be made in subsequent periods, the analysis must involve a "preference for preferences." Some futures must be deemed better than others, and choices in the present will tend to reflect these preferences.

IV.   Past, present, and future

Despite the anticipated continuity of being, the individual knows that the person who will confront the choices in t_1 will be different. This future reality must enter into the decision calculus of the present, in t_0, as a constraint. Within limits, the person who will exist in t_1 can be "constructed" so as to reflect the preference ordering exhibited at t_0 − but only within limits. Such a construction will, at best, be only partial, and the chooser at t_0 will know that the person alive at t_1 must exhibit a will and a personality, a set of preferences, that are "all his own." The new person, emergent only in t_1, may find it in his power to destroy or modify seriously any plans that may be carefully reflected in the forward-looking choices made at t_0. The person who chooses at t_0 operates in a tension that opposes the continuity of his temporal existence as a conscious being to the reckoned potential for temptation by the less reflective other selves that the future may bring forth.

As a continuing conscious being, the individual may be reluctant to impose constraints on his freedom of action. Liberty may be valued even if the person does not know what will be the object of his actions in future periods. At the same time, however, totally unconstrained behavior may be genuinely feared. A preferred life plan is vulnerable to depletion and erosion by patterns of behavior that the "other" persons in future periods may exhibit. From a planning perspective in t_0, therefore, the reference individual may seek out ways to make "subversive" actions costly to those "other persons" that may emerge from the same consciousness in future periods and, in extreme cases, may try to prohibit such behavior.

There are two distinct but related ways the individual might attempt to accomplish this purpose. The first involves the selection of a set of moral precepts that can guide both present- and future-period choices. To the extent that a person establishes a coherent and subjectively meaningful morality, and draws on intellectual and emotional resources in the legitimization and justification of this morality in a manner designed to leave quasi-permanent residues, he will succeed in increasing the costs of any future-period departures from the life plan partially described by adherence to the precepts of such morality. An internal personal commitment to live by a set of moral rules will not explicitly bind choices. But such a commitment can ensure that undesired patterns of behavior (as evaluated from the perspective of t_0) will give rise to feelings of guilt. Consider the work ethic as an example. If a person imbeds this ethic in his psyche, by either design or unconscious habituation, sloth in future periods will be accompanied by subjectively sensed costs. Loafing will seem sinful; it will cost more to loaf.

The person may seek, however, to go beyond an instrumental selection of current-period Z's and also beyond the instrumental adoption of a personal moral code. The individual may, over certain ranges of potential choice behavior, attempt to *precommit* future-period choice by the imposition of binding rules or constraints. That is to say, the person may deliberately reduce the choice options anticipated to be open in t_1 and beyond. There may be a conscious reduction in liberty or freedom of action. The purpose will be to close off possibilities for acting in ways that are deemed "inefficient" in carrying forward a preferred life plan.

As an example, consider Crusoe alone on his island (before Friday). He may deliberately choose to sleep on the beach at a location where the morning tide will rudely awaken him. By sleeping in such a place, Crusoe precommits himself to start the next day's work early. He closes off the option of deciding when to get up because his life plan includes work rather than sloth, and he wants to remove temptation of the latter.

Precommitment has been discussed at some length by Jon Elster in his book *Ulysses and the Sirens*,[4] as the classic example of the title suggests. Ulysses has himself bound to the mast of his ship as it approaches the sirens' shore. He recognizes his weakness of will; he does not trust his ability to resist temptation, and he knows that if he succumbs the larger purpose of the voyage will be undermined.

Precommitment has been analyzed by Thomas Schelling[5] and others as a "strategy of conflict." In potential gamelike interactions, precommitment may offer a means of securing strategic advantage. The general orders the bridge to be burned after his army has crossed the river. Such a strategic "reason of rules" is not the object of our attention in this chapter or, indeed, in this book. In the discussion here, only a single person is directly involved. There is no strategic interaction as such, except that between the person who is and the person who might

---

[4] Jon Elster, *Ulysses and the Sirens* (Cambridge University Press, 1979).

[5] See Thomas Schelling, *The Strategy of Conflict* (Cambridge, Mass.: Harvard University Press, 1960).

be. As the analysis has suggested, constraints on future-period behavior may emerge from the rational calculus of a person who remains totally isolated from other persons. The individual may precommit himself to choices that are deemed more worthy in a long-range perspective than a pattern of purely situational responses.

The analysis is not, of course, restricted to the choice behavior of an individual in social isolation. Part 2 of this chapter extends the analysis to the behavior of the individual in choice settings that are explicitly collective. But even when choice remains strictly "individualistic," the choice setting may be social, as exemplified in market relationships. In these situations, the nonstrategic setting remains descriptive so long as the choice of the individual is not predicted to influence the behavior of other persons directly. Persons who act as demanders and/or suppliers of resources, goods, and services in competitive markets may do so without being conscious that they are bargaining over terms of trade or, differently stated, over shares in the gains from trade. In more general terms, the analysis seems applicable to all large-number settings where the reference person remains one among many and where the behavior of others is taken as a part of the environment rather than as an object to be controlled.

PART 2: INDIVIDUAL PUBLIC CHOICE

I. Introduction

We have discussed the private-choice calculus of the individual in some detail because the analysis is helpful in introducing the more complex calculus of the individual confronting the public- or social-choice setting. In order to reduce the discussion to manageable proportions, we shall ignore several of the complexities that arise. We shall continue to neglect strategic behavior. The individual in a public-choice setting is one among many and can rationally treat the behavior of all others as if it were part of the environment and hence not subject to manipulation. We also continue to concentrate on the choice calculus of a single reference individual. We neglect problems involved in securing agreement among persons, although, as the argument will suggest, the operation of the rules for making arrangements may modify the individual's choice behavior. We presume that the individual will behave in the many-person collective-choice setting as if he pursues his own interests as they are reflected in the underlying utility function.

One reason for the detailed elaboration of private-choice behavior in Part 1 was to suggest that in several respects, the private- and public-choice settings are similar. We can summarize the earlier analysis as follows: A person faces a choice at t_0, a choice that will be constrained by choices made in prior periods; this choice will be informed by the influence that behavior in t_0 is anticipated to exert on choices made in t_1 and beyond. The person in t_1 and beyond is, in part, constructed by choices made in t_0 and earlier, but at the same time the person in t_1 and beyond must be different from the one who must act in t_0. In this setting, the individual chooses among the Z's in t_0; the individual may adopt moral rules; the individual may precommit future choices – all of these actions are designed to further the achievement of a preferred life plan.

II.   Society with a history

Let us now consider the position of an individual who, at t_0, is one among many members of a given society, a community, that has its own history, as a political–collective entity, quite apart from the various collected histories of its individual members. That is to say, the collectivity, as an organized polity, has "acted" over a sequence of past periods. It has gone to war or it has maintained peace; it has imposed onerous taxes on its citizens or it has not; it has allowed citizens to enjoy liberty over wide ranges of possible action or it has not. The "it" that has "acted" to create such a history must, of course, have assumed the form of specific persons who have assumed, captured, or been placed in roles of agents. But these persons as agents will have acted in the name of the collective unit rather than explicitly as identifiable individuals.

The history of the collective unit, described by "choices" taken in all past periods, will constrain the set of available choice options in t_0, those that may be confronted both by the collectivity as such and by the individuals within that collectivity, in a manner fully analogous to the interdependencies discussed in the earlier analysis of private choice. The historically determined constraints may be descriptively summarized in the laws, institutions, customs, and traditions of the community, including the rules or institutions that define the means of making collective "choices." Again, as in the earlier analysis, the "choices" made by the collective unit as such in t_0 will modify the options that will emerge in t_1 and beyond, through influences on the constraints or preferences or both.

Our concern in Part 2 is with the choice behavior of the person who participates in some group decision process as one member (one voter) among many and who expects that his expressed preferences ("choices") will be counted and amalgamated with those of others through the operation of a known rule (e.g., majority or plurality voting) that will generate a single decisive collective outcome that once reached, will be effective for all members, that is, will be "public" in the formal, analytic sense of this term.

III. Temporal interdependence

Faced with a set of collective alternatives or options at t_0, the individual recognizes that both preferences and constraints embodied in the historical record are fixed. These are not within the set of choice variables under the control of the decision makers acting within the decision rules. Existing preference functions and the institutions generated by past choices are "relatively absolute absolutes," subject to change, but only through time — change that might be influenced only marginally by choices made now. In reference to the individual's *own* evaluation of the choice options, there is no difference between private choice and public choice in this respect.

A major difference emerges, however, when the individual recognizes that, for public or collective choice, the possible changes in his own preferences may be irrelevant. Collective decisions are reached through the operation of some rule that combines individual expressions of preference. A preference ordering for the collectivity, treated as a unit, need not correspond to that of any individual in the group and, indeed, may not exist at all.

At this point, the analysis seems to lead naturally into a discussion of the most familiar theorem in social choice, Arrow's impossibility theorem.[6] This theorem shows that, even if individual preference orderings are themselves consistent and do not change through a series of pairwise comparisons between alternatives in the inclusive collective-choice set, the "preference ordering" exhibited by the collectivity, as a unit, may not reflect internal consistency under plausibly acceptable rules for combining individual choices.

The temporal dimension as such is not central to the analysis of the Arrow impossibility theorem, and the whole extended discussion of that theorem has been based on the implicit assumption that all of the pairwise comparisons are contemporaneous. By contrast, our emphasis here is strictly on the time dimension and on its implications for the individual's choice calculus. We are not directly concerned with the possibility of inconsistency in contemporaneous collective "choice," although this possibility might well offer an additional "reason for

[6] See Kenneth J. Arrow, *Social Choice and Individual Values* (New York: Wiley, 1951).

rules," one that we essentially neglect in this book. We are concerned with the attenuation of individual control over collective-choice options and with the effects of such attenuation. A person may exhibit a clear preference between two political-choice options, and the array of separate preferences may be such that the existing decision rule generates a stable result in each discrete time period. Even if the person expects the preferences of others to remain unchanged over a sequence of periods, however, there is no means of predicting whether the sequence of outcomes generated by the decision rule will exhibit a time path that, to this person, seems consistent with his own ordering.

Superficially considered, this result seems to be merely a variant of the impossibility theorem. Note, however, that the problem isolated for examination here is *not* located in the abrupt shiftability in the makeup of majority coalitions (in the absence of single-peakedness in preferences) as in the more familiar contemporaneous setting. The problem here finds its origins in the subjective nature of individual preferences themselves and in the inability of an individual to know *why* other persons order alternatives as they do. An individual may prefer option or candidate A to option or candidate B in t_0 because it is anticipated that the selection of A in t_0 will allow, in time period t_1, a further selection of a_1, which is the ultimately desired objective. Alongside such a person who supports A in t_0, however, there may exist someone else in the decisive coalition who chooses this option for precisely the opposing reason, in order to select a_2 in t_1, a final outcome that the first person may find pessimal rather than optimal.

This fundamental difference between individual calculation in private and public choice has not, to our knowledge, been analyzed. The individual will tend to make voting choices in terms of a shorter time horizon than that reflected in his private choices. The person cannot, by the nature of choice setting itself, incorporate the multiperiod interdependence of decisions to the same degree that is possible in private choice. Although a chooser may recognize, equally in the two settings, that selections made now will influence both preferences and constraints in future periods, the current-period utility value to the individual from "investment" in furthering the achievement of what the same person would prefer the collectivity to become must remain relatively lower than any comparable investment in becoming the private person projected in some idealized life plan. Put in different words, the individual in private choice may try to choose among current-period options so as to construct himself as a continuing consciousness in subsequent periods, as he seeks to achieve a coherent life. The same person, placed as one among many in a public choosing role, must

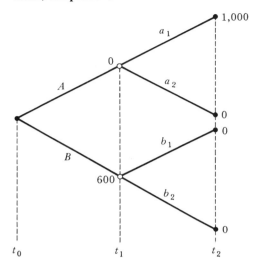

Figure 5.1

exhibit less interest in selecting current options with future periods in prospect.

IV. An illustration

We shall illustrate the difference between private and public choice with a simple example. A person is in a collective-choice setting that presents two options in t_0, one of which will be chosen by the decision rule that combines individual expressions of preference between the two options. Each one of the options is expected to generate results that will be realized in t_1, at which time a second pairwise selection between two later options will be faced. The "choice" emergent from the decision rule in t_1 will, in turn, generate results that will be realized in t_2. We shall truncate the sequence arbitrarily at t_2 for the sake of simplicity.

The individual evaluates the expected payoffs from the perspective at t_0. Figure 5.1 depicts the example in a tree diagram, with specific numerical values for expected payoffs, all of which are evaluated from t_0. The initial options are A and B; which of these will command the expression of preference by our reference person, whose payoffs are as depicted? The "choice" will depend on what the individual predicts the subsequent collective "choice" at t_1 will be. If the setting were purely private, with identical payoffs, the person would know that control over the options at t_1 would remain internal. Hence, a reasonably high probability would be placed on the choice of a_1 at t_1, so as to allow the ultimate achievement of the highest present-valued payoff of 1,000. Despite the recognition that the person at t_1 will be different from the chooser at t_0, the latter's subjective sense of continuity will make such a probability assessment rational. If the setting were one of private choice, therefore, A would be selected over B in t_0.

The postulated setting is one in which the individual is one among many, however, and the decision is to be made for the collectivity as a unit, with the results applicable to all persons in the community. We are concerned with how the individual will express a preference between A and B in the voting booth at t_0.

Our reference person may well vote for B rather than A in t_0, reversing the revealed preference that might be exhibited in the private-choice setting. He may take this action because of his inability to place a high probability on the prospect that the collectivity, as a unit and via the operation of the existing decision rule, will, when faced with the options a_1 and a_2 at t_1, select the a_1 option, the result indicated to be the most desirable to the person in question. There is here no continuity of consciousness, no sense of quasi-permanent psychological unity. Even if the voter-chooser at t_0 reckons that there will be no change in individual preference orderings, either in his own or in those of others, between the two time periods, a lower probability must be placed on the prospect that the decision rule will generate the most desirable result in t_1. This lower probability stems from the fact that the individual has no way of knowing why others, who may be partners in the coalition that might express preferences for A in t_0, order the options predicted to be faced at t_1. Persons in such a prospective coalition may well order the alternatives in Figure 5.1 in precisely opposed fashion to the person whose payoffs are depicted.

To make our example even more specific, consider a risk-neutral voter in the large-number setting who has no knowledge of the preferences of others. Under simple majority voting rules, this voter will assign a .5 prospect to each alternative at each stage in the pairwise choice sequence. In the numerical example of Figure 5.1, the individual will then vote for B over A, despite the fact that the present value of the sequence Aa_1 is higher than that of any other. If B is chosen, the individual enjoys the payoff of 600 units at t_1. By contrast, if A is selected by the decision rule, there is only a .5 prospect that t_1 having been reached, the rule will generate a_1 at the critical second node.

A more general way of stating the central proposition of the analysis is to say that the individual participant in collective choice will find it difficult to make *instrumental* use of the collectivity in the furtherance of genuinely long-term objectives. "Investmentlike" collective alternatives will tend to be placed lower than "consumptionlike" alternatives in individual orderings. This basic reason for the limited time perspective exhibited in collective or public choice is quite different from other, more familiar reasons having to do with electoral term limits and the nonmarketability of individualized shares in "public good."

V.   Moral rules and/or constitutional commitment

In Part 1 of this chapter we demonstrated that the individual who recognizes the temporal interdependence of choice may find it rational to adopt a set of moral rules even with reference to purely private behavior. It should be clear, however, that moral rules designed to constrain future-period behavior become enormously more important in the collective setting. The reference person knows that he is only one member of a group and that collective outcomes emerge from the operation of a specified decision structure. How can limits be placed on the "behavior" of the collectivity as a unit? How can the individual act in t_0 to ensure personal survival and security in the many-person world? He will seek to influence not primarily his own behavior in future periods but that of others who will be or will become members of the choosing group. With these considerations the individual may, on quite rational grounds, invest current-period resources in the indoctrination, dissemination, and transmission of a set of general principles or rules that will, generally, influence behavior toward patterns of situational response that are predictably bounded.

We also suggested in Part 1 that an awareness of the multiperiod interdependence of choice may sometimes provide a basis for precommitment, even in the most isolated private-choice setting. The individual may not trust himself as a rational chooser in any moment other than the reflective present. As we indicated, however, there are natural limits on precommitment in private choice, since the individual knows that his own freedom of action is to be constrained.

In a public-choice setting, no such natural limits apply, and the individual has immensely stronger grounds for choosing to impose constitutional precommitments on the behavior of collective entities. As noted earlier in Part 2, the individual at t_0 is less capable of predicting the collective response to the choice options predicted to be confronted in future periods than of predicting private, personal reactions. In the former, even if the individual predicts his own preferences accurately, there must remain uncertainty about the response patterns of others. As a general principle, rationality precepts should dictate an inverse relationship between the predictability of future-period "choices" and the desirability of constraining the set of future-period options.[7]

A second and related argument supports the relatively greater attractiveness of constraints on future-period choices in the collective setting. In strictly private choice, as noted earlier, the individual knows that any precommitment binds his ability to satisfy personal preferences, whatever these may be. There is a trade-off between precommitment and liberty. By contrast, in the public-choice setting, no such trade-off exists, at least in any direct sense. In voting for limits on future-period choice options open to the collectivity as a unit, the individual need not think in terms of restricting the set of personally preferred options at all. The boundaries imposed on the ranges of collective "choices" may be treated as being outside any set of potentially desired outcomes. Such boundaries may be considered applicable only to the potential collective outcomes that might be generated from the expressed preferences of persons other than the reference individual. Clearly, constitutional constraints on the collectivity's power to act will tend to be treated quite differently than possible precommitments on private behavior.[8]

Let us return to the example depicted in Figure 5.1. The individual will tend to support a constitutional constraint that will increase the probability that the collectivity, when and if t_1 is reached, will generate the a_1 rather than the a_2 outcome. With such a constraint in place, the individual might select A rather than B in t_0, even in the public-choice setting. Consider, as a practical example, a collective choice between paying off and not paying off outstanding public debt. The individual may well express a preference for repayment, hence reducing future tax burdens associated with debt service, *if* he can be assured constitutionally or otherwise that new debt will not be issued once the old debt is

---

[7] Ron Heiner has developed a theory of constraints based on the predicted vulnerability of actors to false interpretations of signals. The analysis is extended to behavioral rigidities in nonhuman species. See Heiner's "Uncertainty, Rules, and Behavior: A Theory of Behavior and Evolution as the Resistance to Unreliable Complexity" (Brigham Young University, 1981, mimeographed).

[8] The relationship works both ways, of course. Although, as suggested, an individual may be more willing to impose limits on the range of collective outcomes as a means of securing protection against the impositions of others, the same individual may, and for much the same reasons, be more willing to use the agency of the state as a means of imposing his will on others. The reformers who secured adoption of the constitutional prohibition on the use of alcohol in the United States did not consider themselves to be restricting their own behavior.

retired. Failing such assurance, the individual may express preference for continued rollover of the old debt.

Constitutional commitments or constraints become means by which members of a polity can incorporate long-term considerations into current-period decisions. In the absence of such constraints, individuals will be led, almost necessarily, to adopt a short-term perspective in politics. We shall discuss some of the practical implications of this short-term perspective in Chapter 6.

Politics without rules, I: Time and nonconstrained collective action

I. Introduction

In the preceding chapter, we attempted to demonstrate that individual behavior in collective choice is likely to reflect shorter time horizons than comparable behavior in private or individualized choice, and for individually rational reasons. The person who may be willing to wait privately, to behave with prudence in order that he or his heirs may secure the fruits of long-term investment in human or nonhuman capital may, at the same time, be unwilling to wait collectively, as reflected in expressions through political decision-making institutions. Because of the necessary attenuation of individually identifiable rights or shares in the fruits of collective or governmental "investment," individual time horizons in politics are shortened. If this underlying hypothesis is valid, it would follow that as modern societies have become increasingly collectivized or politicized, there has been a shift toward a higher discount rate implicit in the allocation of the economy's resources.

In this chapter we shift our attention to the less abstract and more practical level of real-world politics. But we should stress that we do not go all the way; we dare not enter the realm of historical or descriptive institutional detail. In a sense, our discussion remains abstract in that we examine the predicted workings of idealized models of politics in democracies as these models might be expected to work in confrontation with the problems of modern experience. Analytic models of politics assist us in understanding why these familiar problems persist in modern political life. Such an understanding, however, is a by-product of the primary function of the analysis here, which is to offer support for constitutional rules or constraints on practical political grounds.

Our purpose is to develop the intertemporal theme with the aid of distinct and familiar examples drawn from economic problems of the 1970s and 1980s in the United States and other Western nations. We shall discuss the "high-tax trap," the "inflation trap," and the "public-debt trap," all of which demonstrate the general problem of imprudence in modern democratic polities, different countries having experienced these separate problems in differing degrees of relative importance. The inferences to be drawn for our larger and more comprehensive theme become clear as the analysis is developed; governments can be induced to take the long view only if they are appropriately constrained by constitutional rules that do not now exist. These reasons for rules emerge from an understanding of the workings of modern political economies.

II.   The social discount rate

The discussion in this chapter is related to a long-continuing topic in the theory of economic policy, often treated under the rubric of "social discount rate." Traditionally, and especially since Pigou's *Economics of Welfare*, published early in this century,[1] economists have concerned themselves with the normative question, At what rate "should" society discount the future? How "should" the utility of future generations be weighted in the making of present-period decisions? More particularly, economists have asked, Is the interest of future generations sufficiently weighted by discounting at the market-determined rate of return on capital investment, the rate that market institutions install as a parameter for private-investment decisions? Should the collectivity as such make its own investment decisions on the basis of the market-determined rate of discount, and if the market rate is "too high," should the collectivity, as a unit, replace the market behavior of individuals in all or in part of the investment or capital accumulation activity of the society?

These questions are intrinsically interesting, but for our purposes the implicit assumptions that prompted economists to ask them are more revealing. Almost without exception, the economists who asked these questions assumed that once a satisfactory normative solution could be agreed on, a benevolent government could, and presumably would, implement this solution. Never once did these economists pause to ask themselves whether government, as it is actually observed to operate, could or would implement the "optimal" discount rate that emerges from the careful exercise in normative prescription. In other words, the welfare theorists worked without a positive theory or model of governmental–political behavior, either implicit or explicit.

"Public choice," the area of research with which we have long been associated, emerged in the 1950s, 1960s, and 1970s to fill this truly awesome gap in normative analysis. Within properly defined limits and appropriately qualified, public choice does offer a positive theory of

[1] A. C. Pigou, *The Economics of Welfare*, 4th ed. (London: Macmillan, 1932).

how politics works or, stated somewhat differently, offers a panoply of theories about the working of politics under different sets of postulated rules and institutions. It is on this analytic structure that our conclusion about the political discount rate is grounded. The "social discount rate" generated in the operation of modern political decision-making institutions will be higher than that rate of time preference exhibited by persons in their private behavior. This statement takes the form of a testable hypothesis; it is not a normative proposition. It may well be that persons exhibit personal time preferences in market behavior that are "too high" when judged against some extraindividual criterion. To make such an argument one must resort to value norms that are not necessary in making the positive statement about relative discount rates in market and political behavior. We can say that the discount rate embodied in the political process is higher than that embodied in the operation of the competitive market without invoking our own private variant of a social welfare function.

III.   The high-tax trap

The three main examples we shall introduce are familiar from economic policy discussions of the early 1980s. The "high-tax trap" is a term we shall use to refer to the set of considerations often summarized under "supply-side economics." Our analysis of this trap, or dilemma, offers a basis for imposing limits on the government's taxing authority, even in a setting where the taxpayer and the beneficiary groups are largely coincident in membership.[2] That is to say, we model government democratically in the sense that it is presumed to be responsive to the demands of citizens both for expanded state services (and transfers) and for lower tax rates. The dilemma emerges here from the disparity in time horizons between the two separate sets of behavior, private and political.

Is it possible to say that tax rates are "too high" except by reference to some value-laden normative criterion that suggests the existence of some "optimal" size of public or governmental outlay relative to the private or market sector of an economy? In a nonevaluative sense,

---

[2] The basis for imposing tax limits that emerges from the argument here is quite different from the one we offered on the basis of a contrasting political model in our earlier book, *The Power to Tax* (Cambridge University Press, 1979). There, we stated that taxes tend to be "too high" because of the revenue-maximizing proclivities of government, which was modeled as one player in a two-player game with taxpayers. In that analysis, there was no dilemma aspect such as is examined here, and the set of questions concerning the time horizon for adjustment did not arise.

we could say that taxes are "too high" only if everyone expressed agreement on such a proposition, with members of the government (politicians, legislators, and bureaucrats) as well as direct beneficiaries included in the group. But surely the members of the group, the recipients of net transfers in particular, would never agree to any reduction in the size of the public sector, as measured by the amount of outlay and, indirectly, by tax revenues. So it would seem. Without some normative standard for judgment, we would never expect to obtain general agreement on the proposition that governmental outlays are too high.

This proposition is not, however, the same as the statement that tax *rates* are "too high." It is at least logically possible that tax rates may be so high that tax *revenues* are actually lower than they would be at *lower* rates. In this case, of course, there should be general agreement among all parties on the need for a rate reduction, if not a revenue reduction.

The simple arithmetical relationship between tax rates and total tax revenues came to be widely discussed under the "Laffer curve" rubric in the early 1980s in the United States, since the relationship was brought into political prominence by Professor Arthur Laffer. As many critics pointed out, the relationship was articulated in writings as far back as the time of the Moors, and possibly even the early Greeks. And, indeed, there is little more to the relationship as such than the mathematical properties of a simple functional form. Some such relationship must exist so long as *any* inverse behavioral response of taxpayers to tax rates is predicted.

Pointing out that such a rate—revenue relationship must exist, however, is not the same as suggesting that modern fiscal systems are described by locations on the "wrong," or inverse, portion of the schedule or curve, that is, at a position where a decrease in tax rates would increase rather than decrease tax revenues. In some of the journalistic advocacy of "supply-side economics" in the United States of the early 1980s, the arguments seemed to suggest that this position was, indeed, characteristic of the existing fiscal structure.

The initial reaction of public-choice economists is surely to reject the behavioral model that would be required to generate such a position. It would seem impossible that any rationally motivated governmental decision process could have allowed tax rates to reach such levels. Why would rates have been allowed to become so high as to reduce total tax revenues, since such rates would not be to the advantage of taxpayers, program beneficiaries, or politicians? It would seem to be in no group's interest to sustain such a fiscal structure. Behaviorally, location along the inverse segment of the relevant rate—revenue curve seems bizarre, quite apart from the limited results of empirical studies that also suggest response elasticities that fall far short of those required to generate such results.

The initial reaction of the public-choice economists may, however, be less definitive than at first it seems, and a more sophisticated examination of the political decision matrix within which tax and outlay decisions are made, along with an analysis of individual responses to these decisions, might suggest a plausible scenario that might well produce the position on the "wrong" side of the rate−revenue relationship. The central element in this scenario is the disparity in time horizons between private and public choice.

Let us assume, possibly as a counterfactual, that the fiscal structure is in the position indicated. There is an inverse relationship between tax rates and total tax revenues. Is there any behaviorally meaningful path through which the system might have reached this position?

Let us look first at the utility or preference functions of those who participate in the process from which governmental fiscal decisions emerge. We can, at one extreme, think of all fiscal decisions as being produced by the operation of majority voting rules, with all members of the community equally franchised to participate in the determination of the outcomes. The analysis is sufficiently general, however, to allow for differential powers of collective influence among different groups of constituents. In any case, those persons who participate in the making of collective decisions will wish to make outlays or expenditures through the political unit. They will need such expenditures either to finance "good things" (governmentally financed goods and services and transfers) and/or to line their own pockets or those of their friends and constituents. In either case, we can stipulate that funds, or *revenues*, are desired by those who participate in collective decision making. Revenues are "goods" in the utility functions of persons who ultimately make fiscal choices, whoever these persons may be.

At the same time, however, the levy of taxes is required for the acquisition of these revenues. (We shall, in this section, ignore the prospects of revenue generation through either money creation or debt issue; these prospects will be discussed in the two following sections.) In some way or another, funds must be extracted from citizens in their private economic roles or capacities. This taxing process will be painful, regardless of the model of governmental decision making that is postulated. In utility-function terminology, taxes or tax rates become "bads" rather than "goods." In some Utopian sense, persons in collective-decision roles would ideally prefer to spend without having to levy taxes. And the worst of all worlds for these persons would be some requirement that taxes be imposed without any accompanying outlay of funds on desired programs. These results remain true whether or not the taxpayer and the beneficiary groups are fully, partially, or not at all coincident in membership.

Note that to this point, we have said nothing at all about the time dimension. We have not *dated* the revenue flows the government expects to receive as a result of the imposition of a tax or an increase in the tax rate. We now postulate that those who participate in collective decision making are motivated by short-term considerations, for reasons analyzed in the previous chapter. By "short term" in this application, we mean that fiscal decisions are considered with reference to a time period shorter than that relevant to the private or individualized adjustments to tax-rate changes. We do not need to define the time horizon that informs individual collective choice in more detail than this; we require only that the effective time horizon embodied in governmental fiscal decisions be less extensive than that embodied in taxpayer response to tax-rate changes.

We know, of course, that taxpayer adjustments to tax-rate changes take time. In response to rate increases, persons must seek out and find nontaxable substitutes for the tax base, or at least substitutes that are taxed at differentially lower rates, whether the tax is imposed on a source or a use of income. Persons must shift investment to non-taxed or low-taxed opportunities and must invest in opportunities that are complementary to those directly advantaged. Individuals must learn about, and take advantage of, legal loopholes, which may have to be invented by lawyers and accountants. The whole analysis here depends only on the plausible assumption that in considering the revenue potential of a tax or tax-rate increase, the participant in governmental decision making operates on the basis of a shorter time perspective (a higher discount rate) than the one that describes the adjustment of persons as taxpayers to a post-tax equilibrium.

For simplicity, let us postulate that full adjustment to a tax-rate change takes ten years, a period of adjustment that has been informally estimated to be relevant in modern fiscal systems of Western nations. Let us postulate, furthermore, that the time horizon effectively informing the behavior of participants in the making of collective political decisions on taxes (and spending) is five years or less. There are, of course, many reasons to support this postulated disparity in the time perspective for the individuals in the two separate roles, only one of which was discussed at some length in the previous chapter.

Given the postulated discrepancy in time horizons, "political equilibrium" will be established before "taxpayer equilibrium." That is to say, the individual as a participant in the political decision-making process will try to attain a position where the trade-offs between tax rates and tax revenues faced in fiscal reality, over the relevant time period, are equated with the subjective trade-offs between these two arguments in the utility function. So long as the individual, as a fiscal decision maker, values the "good" measured by increased funds higher than the "bad" measured by the tax rates required to generate such funds, he will "vote for" or support increases in tax rates. Both of these variables will be measured with respect to the period of time over which the funds are anticipated to provide benefits and without direct regard to the period of time that might be required for full taxpayer adjustments. As such, these individual participants in fiscal decision-making processes will be uninterested in the fact that taxpayers will take ten years to attain full equilibrium adjustment to the current tax rates, even when, at another level of consciousness, they may realize that they are the same persons who are involved in the quite separate roles. As political decision makers, individuals are concerned with the flow of revenues from taxes, and with the program benefits therefrom, only for a period of five years or less.

In the illustration here, however, taxpayers will not have made the full behavioral adjustment within five years. From this result follows the simple fact that the government can expect to collect *more* revenues per period at any given tax rate (above some initial starting rate) within a five-year period than it can expect to collect over the full ten-year sequence.[3] Hence, the fiscal process that embodies the shorter time horizon will exploit taxpayers more fully than would a process embodying a time horizon equal to, or longer than, the period of taxpayer adjustment. Taxpayers can be squeezed more fully by a governmental decision process that reflects interest in short-run revenue flows than by a process that incorporates a genuinely long-term perspective. As a familiar nontax example, the OPEC oil cartel was able to exploit oil consumers more before individuals adjusted the size and efficiency of the vehicle fleet than it was able to do after the adjustment took place.

Given sufficient time, of course, taxpayers will adjust to any given tax rate, and the coincidence of political and taxpayer equilibrium must ultimately be attained. In this full equilibrium, two separate conditions must be met. The trade-offs within the calculus of the persons who participate in governmental decision making must be equal, and tax-

---

[3] In terms of simple geometry, this result becomes immediately apparent. Although we shall not depict it here, the short-run "Laffer," or rate–revenue, curve above the initial tax rate will always lie outside the long-run, or full-adjustment, curve.

payers must be fully adjusted to the current tax rate. Such a full-equilibrium position might well be located in the range of the *long-term* rate–revenue schedule where rates and revenues are inversely related, although the precise location would have to be empirically determined. But the analysis suggests that because the long-term relationship is irrelevant to the political decision process, the generation of a position on the inverse segment of this relationship or schedule is not "collectively irrational," in that there need be no violation of the precepts of rationality by those who participate in political decision making.

If, however, such a position were reached, and if it were recognized as such, why would political decision makers not react by reducing tax rates? The answer is the reverse side of the tax-rate increase coin. By cutting tax rates, government would find revenues reduced in the time period relevant to those who participate in political decision making. Even a shared presumption that a reduction in tax rates would generate an increased stream of revenues per period, after, say, ten years, would not affect the decision of those who, by our postulate, remain interested in revenue flows only over a five-year sequence. The maintenance of high tax rates would ensure higher revenues over this relevant period. The revenue-enhancing effects of a possible tax cut are long run, not short run.

Within the time perspective of the early 1980s, the critics who opposed the naïve supply-side economic arguments were correct. Tax-rate cuts were predicted to and did reduce revenue flows; budget deficits were increased, especially since outlays were cut very little, if at all. Whether the critics would have been correct within a time horizon allowing for full taxpayer adjustment will never be known, because pressures for tax-rate increases, for short-term revenue reasons, emerged as early as 1982.

This is the setting for what we call the "high-tax trap." Individuals who participate in the making of political decisions cannot, even if they fully understand the situation they are in, readily escape from this dilemma. Given the absence of constraints on the fiscal proclivities of the collectivity, along with the existing rules and procedures for generating fiscal decisions, the individual who adopts a genuinely long term perspective in his role as a participant in politics is behaving irrationally. In this setting, the argument for binding constraints on governmental fiscal authority becomes evident. Only if some means can be found to limit the ability of governments (political coalitions) in subsequent periods to depart from a reflectively evaluated and presently preferred long-term fiscal program will the individual participant find it advantageous to support the separate elements in such a program. Only through constitutional change can the institutions of modern politics be adjusted to ensure that, within these institutions, persons will have incentives to act in accordance with what they recognize to be the long-term interest of the community, as well as their own.[4]

IV.   The inflation trap

There are many similarities between the high-tax trap and the inflation trap, which we shall analyze in this section. The similarities are readily explained once it is recognized that both traps have essentially the same behavioral basis, which we have summarized as the disparity between the discount rate embodied in the choices made by individuals in their separate roles as public and private decision makers.

The United States, along with other Western countries, found itself caught up in an inflation in the 1970s that seemed to be continuing unabated. The inflation persisted despite the widespread recognition that a national economy operates less efficiently under an inflationary than a noninflationary regime. In a long-term perspective, inflation is clearly not in the interest of any group. But the short-term perspective that informs the decision calculus of those who participate in politics seemed to prevent them from initiating the action that would have been required to restore effective monetary stability.

How did we get into the dilemma? Is there a way out that can be other than temporary? An answer to the first question, which is perhaps essential to any attempt to answer the second, requires that we summarize the history of ideas in economics, at least since the impact of Lord Keynes. We shall do nothing more than sketch the bare outlines.

Keynes was successful in imposing on the mind-set of economists of the middle years of this century an abstract model of a high-unemployment, underutilized economy. And Keynes was surely correct when he noted that the ideas of academicians ultimately influence the actions of politicians. In the initial Keynesian model, demand brings forth supply, and increases in demand sop up underutilized manpower and capital, without creating increases in costs and prices. There are no supply-side constraints in the model, and quite literally, public spending is costless in terms of effectively displaced alternatives.

---

[4] In collaboration with a colleague, one of us has developed the "high-tax trap" analysis in some detail. See James M. Buchanan and Dwight R. Lee, "Tax Rates and Tax Revenues in Political Equilibrium," *Economic Inquiry* 20 (July 1982): 344–54; "Politics, Time and the Laffer Curve," *Journal of Political Economy* 90 (August 1982); 816–19; and "The Simple Analytics of the Laffer Curve" (paper presented at the 38th Congress of the International Institute of Public Finance, Copenhagen, August 1982).

This simple model appeared in the textbooks of all economics students after World War II, including all of those who later became the political leaders and opinion molders of the 1960s and 1970s. And surprisingly, the simple Keynesian model remains in many of the textbooks of the 1980s.

As early as the 1950s, however, there were indications that the Keynesian model is wrong in a critical respect. Supply schedules are not flat, to revert to familiar geometrical reference. Supply curves slope upward. Increases in demand, even in an economy with some or even considerable unused capacity, generate pressures on costs and hence on prices, at least in some sectors, especially if monetary policy is accommodating. This newly found post-Keynesian relationship between inflation and the rate of unemployment was accepted as an empirical reality of the late 1950s and 1960s. Its definitive version was presented by A. W. Phillips in 1958.[5]

The "Phillips curve" dominated macroeconomic policy discussion during the 1960s. This curve, or relationship, depicts the trade-off between unemployment, on the one hand, and the rate of inflation, on the other. The central idea is that a positive rate of inflation generates a reduction in the rate of unemployment (or an increase in employment). Once the existence of such a trade-off was accepted by economists, they began to temper their earlier enthusiasm for continued increases in aggregate demand to stimulate the economy, but they stayed within the broadly defined Keynesian model by talking about an "optimal" rate of inflation, based on the notion that optimality is attained when the trade-off between inflation and unemployment in the utility function of the political decision maker matches that dictated by the Phillips relationship. A little inflation seemed to be but a small price to pay for increased employment and output.

Things did not quite work out as the economists of the 1960s had foreseen. What the Phillips curve macroeconomists failed to reckon with was the time dimension of the inflation−unemployment trade-off. To be sure, there was empirical evidence that an increase in the rate of unanticipated inflation could generate a temporary increase in employment (a reduction in unemployment). But after a time, employment (and unemployment) seemed to settle back to a natural rate, a rate that was not basically affected by the now anticipated rate of inflation but that was, instead, dependent on structural characteristics

---

[5] A. W. Phillips, "The Relation Between Unemployment and the Rate of Change in Money Wage Rates in the United Kingdom, 1861−1957," *Economica* 25 (November 1958): 283−99.

of the economy, on such things as the flexibility of labor markets, the spatial location of employment, the skill level of particular employee groups, minimum wage and union restrictions, levels of unemployment, disability, retirement compensation, and a host of like factors. Economists came slowly to learn that no permanent and continuing increase in employment could be sustained by some optimally chosen and maintained rate of inflation.

At this point in our potted macroeconomic history, however, public-choice economists had something to contribute. Once those who participated in the making of governmental decisions had been led to think that a little inflation was the route to higher employment, even if such stimulus proved to be temporary, the same individuals were tempted to repeat the exercise, generating a second round of inflation in exchange for a second short-term, or temporary, increase in employment and output in the economy. The simple logic of short-run response built into the political mechanism seemed to suggest that politically induced inflation would accelerate, at least for many rounds of adjustment.

Such was the state of the macroeconomic game, so to speak, until the mid-1970s. Since the late 1970s, however, more sophisticated models of political–economic interaction have been developed. These models indicate that there may emerge a political–economic equilibrium closely akin to that discussed earlier under the high-tax trap. Politically induced inflation need not continue to accelerate to levels of hyper-inflation. A political equilibrium may be reached well short of such levels. An equilibrium of this sort will be attained when the internal trade-off of the participant in political decisions, which embodies the short-term perspective of modern democracy, matches the inflation–employment trade-off dictated by the short-term Phillips relationship, while at the same time the inflation rate is fully anticipated, ensuring that the solution satisfies the long-term Phillips relationship.[6]

Such a full political equilibrium necessarily satisfies the conditions of the Phillips relationship for both the short and the long term. That is to say, unemployment is at its "natural rate," but there is also a continuing and fully anticipated inflation. In such an equilibrium, there is no longer any short-term incentive for the governmental decision maker to generate more inflation, and furthermore, individuals are fully adjusted to the rate of inflation that exists.

Unemployment at this full equilibrium is as high, or possibly even higher, than it would be if there were no inflation at all. To the extent

---

[6] See Finn E. Kydland and Edward C. Prescott, "Rules Rather Than Discretion: The Inconsistency of Optimal Plans," *Journal of Political Economy* 85 (June 1977): 473–91.

that inflation creates any inefficiency in the economy, the full equilibrium seems clearly to be nonoptimal. It would seem to be in the interests of all persons to reduce or to eliminate the rate of inflation.

A trap exists, however, because any reduction in the anticipated rate of inflation will, according to the short-term Phillips relationship, generate short-term increases in unemployment, as, indeed, the United States witnessed in serious fashion in 1981 and 1982. The participant in political decision making will not normally base decisions on a time horizon sufficiently long to make the reduction or elimination of inflation rational, even if the long-term benefits of such action are completely recognized.

In such a setting, the incentives of the participant in politics can be modified so as to ensure choices based on a long-term perspective only if the discretionary authority of the collectivity is restricted. The political decision maker can act with prudence in investing in long-term disinflation only if he can be assured that political coalitions, in subsequent periods, will not reinflate in response to short-term utility considerations. This general point was widely recognized in the macroeconomic policy discussions in the United States in the early 1980s. But there seemed to be a surprising failure to draw the proper inferences to the effect that constitutional limits on the monetary authority of the collectivity are necessary to resolve the dilemma.

V.   The public-debt trap

Our discussion of the public-debt trap will be brief, since this trap is in most respects identical with the two macroeconomic applications of the public–private discount rate disparity already examined. In analyzing the high-tax trap, we neglected public debt as a source of revenues. The introduction of the public-borrowing option clearly expands the possibility frontier of the participant in political choice.

Even if the effects of public-debt issue are recognized by *all* members of the polity (which seems a highly questionable assumption, although it is not vital to our argument here), the shortened time horizon in politics will make this financing option preferable to taxation over some initial ranges of outlay unless there are constitutional or moral prohibitions on debt issue. By borrowing the funds with which to finance currently enjoyed "goods," the participant is postponing the day of payment. Governments can borrow at or below the market-determined rate of interest. But the discount rate that informs politics is higher than the market rate of interest, for reasons already discussed. Hence, the short-term benefits expected from outlays will exceed the short-term costs computed as the present values of anticipated future tax payments discounted at market rates. This calculus remains valid even for the person who realizes that in the long run, a debt-free fiscal structure is preferable to a debt-ridden structure. By forgoing the benefits of debt-financed current spending, however, the person is not able to insure against the long-term tax liability that debt service and amortization imply. A political coalition in periods subsequent to that in which current fiscal choices must be made may wholly undo any effects of current-period fiscal prudence. There is simply no rational basis for an individual to support, to "vote for," fiscal prudence in the operation of ordinary democratic politics. Public debt will tend to be overextended relative to any plausible long-term arguments for the use of this fiscal instrument. The political equilibrium between debt and tax finance will be distorted in favor of debt, and tax rates will be excessive for the reasons already analyzed, at least by the criterion of the long-term interests of the members of the community.

Precisely the same logic applies, of course, to the possible repayment or retirement of an existing public debt. The participant in ordinary politics may recognize that debt retirement now will benefit the whole community in the long run, but given nonfiscally constrained democratic decision processes, there is no means of guaranteeing that debt retirement now will, indeed, have the long-term effects that are preferred.

As in the two previous examples, incentives that will induce the individual, as a participant in politics, to behave in accordance with his (and the community's) long-term interest can be provided only through some limitation on the powers of political coalitions (governments) to offset or destroy the effects of long-term "investmentlike" choices that might be made currently.[7]

VI.   Other examples

Through the analysis of three familiar policy issues from the macroeconomics of the 1980s, we have presented the public–private time discount disparity in stark and simple form. Many other examples could be examined outside the macroeconomic area of inquiry, but only a few will be noted in passing here.

---

[7] For analysis of the debt dilemma along lines that are in many respects similar to those presented here, see James M. Buchanan, "Debt, Demos, and the Welfare State" (paper presented at a conference on the welfare state, Civitas, Gesellschaft zur Förderung von Wissenschaft und Kunst, Munich, West Germany, October 1983).

The "punishment dilemma" and the "Samaritan's dilemma" were examined by one of us in earlier writings.[8] Neither of these focuses directly on the time discount discrepancy. Both, however, illustrate the temporal dimensionality issue and point to the need for imposing commitments. In the punishment dilemma, a short-term utility-maximizing strategy dictates weighting the disutility of the punishee or criminal much more heavily than any long-term maximizing strategy would suggest. As a result of short-term maximization, policy tends to "coddle criminals"; crime increases, and we suffer the long-term consequences. A genuinely long-term perspective would suggest increases in both the certainty and severity of punishment, but unless participants in democratic politics could be assured that future political coalitions would not reverse current reforms, the necessary costs of imposing such reforms would continue to outweigh the benefits promised in the longer term.

In the Samaritan's dilemma, much of the problem of the modern welfare state is explained. A short-term maximizing strategy calls for heeding the obvious sufferings, here and now, of those observed to be needy. Such strategy calls for the financing of assistance, despite the recognition that increased transfer payments generate long-term increases in the number of indigents. A strategy of austerity with respect to eligibility for transfers would increase the ranks of the self-reliant in the long run. But unless the individual who participates in politics today can be assured that such a strategy will be adhered to in the future, the austerity policy applied today may seem unduly callous and cruel.

VII. Conclusions

In this chapter, primarily through the use of three applications from macroeconomic policy, we have tried to demonstrate in practical and relevant terms the basic logic of, or reason for, the imposition of binding constraints or rules on the activities of collective units or governments. The theme of the disparity between the rate of time discount applied in public and in private choice, possibly by the same person, has been used to show that the political concentration on temporary or short-term benefits, a concentration that is inherent in the structure of unconstrained majoritarian politics and also in other

---

[8] See James M. Buchanan, *The Limits of Liberty* (University of Chicago Press, 1975), ch. 8; and *Freedom in Constitutional Contract* (College Station: Texas A & M University Press, 1977), ch. 12.

nonconstrained govermental decision-making procedures, to the relative neglect of long-term considerations, may produce results that are desired by no person or group of persons in the community — hence, the use of the word "trap" or "dilemma." In short, the results produced by the short-term perspective in modern politics may be "Pareto pessimal."

CHAPTER 7

Rules and justice

I. Introduction

"Justice" is a familiar value — if an obscure one in much modern discussion. In this chapter, our purpose is to explore the connection between justice and rules and to offer an understanding of the concept of justice that is both coherent and consistent with the broad constitutionalist—contractarian thrust of our position. Our specific claim is that justice takes its meaning from the rules of the social order within which notions of justice are to be applied. To appeal to considerations of justice is to appeal to relevant rules. Talk of justice without reference to those rules is meaningless. If this claim is accepted, it follows that an acknowledgment of justice as a value carries with it, in and of itself, a *reason* for rules.

In one sense, this emphasis stands much modern discussion of the relationship between justice and rules on its head. Usually, justice is taken to provide an independent norm in terms of which alternative rules or acts can be evaluated. That is to say, orthodox discussion has been preoccupied with the "justice of rules." Under our alternative conceptualization, rules become the basis of justice: Rules are logically prior.

It is useful to make, at the outset, a distinction between the notion of "just conduct," on the one hand, and the notion of "just rules," on the other. The former involves justice *within* rules; it deals with justice as a criterion for evaluating behavior within an institutional setting defined by preexisting rules. The latter involves justice *among* rules; it deals with justice as a criterion for evaluating alternative sets of rules. Although we shall draw this distinction sharply, part of our argument here is that justice as a means of evaluating rules can be usefully viewed as an example of justice *within* rules. That is, the notion of just conduct — not the notion of just rules — is the central one in our argument. The question of just rules is, we shall argue, appropriately treated as a particular instance of justice *within* rules.

How, then, is "just conduct" to be defined? Just conduct consists of behavior that does not violate rules to which one has given prior consent. The role of consent involves, as a central piece, the proposition that agreement, either implicit or explicit, is required to legitimize rules. Rules, so legitimized, then become the reference point against which the justice of individuals' behavior can be assessed.

Once this view is taken, justice is seen to be not so much an external criterion for the evaluation of alternative rules and/or social orders as an intrinsic part of the relevant rule structure. Considerations of justice argue not so much for a wholesale reconstruction and reformation of rules as for a proper understanding of which rules actually prevail and for a reconciliation of conflicts, inconsistencies, and ambiguities among those prevailing rules. Justice is seen to demand a harmonization of the rules and possibly an extension of the domain of rule-governed behavior. Justice is not, however, seen to provide an independent norm on the basis of which ab initio design of ideal rules might be structured. It is *consensus* that performs that basic normative function. In our conceptualization, rules set the terms of justice, rather than the reverse. For this reason, justice takes on a certain "nonteleological," history-dependent cast. It is no longer possible to give an account of what justice entails − in terms either of conduct or of the nature of rules − that is entirely general, abstract, and decontextualized. What justice requires depends on what particular rules individuals happen to have agreed to.

We shall begin our discussion with the issue of justice within rules − of what it means to behave justly in the context of a well-established institutional order. In Section III, we shall attempt to explain why considerations of justice, in terms of obedience to prevailing rules, have moral force, more or less whatever those rules happen to be. In Sections IV and V, we shall extend the discussion to the question of justice among rules.

II.   Just conduct and the notion of desert

What does just conduct entail? A common response to this question is that justice consists in persons' being given their "due": It is just that each receives whatever he deserves. At first sight, this response seems to beg all the relevant questions; to say that justice is a matter of persons' being given their deserts can be meaningful only to the extent that their deserts can be independently determined. What exactly, one may ask, does desert entail? How does it arise?

To pose such questions is, however, to begin inquiry in the wrong place − with the most difficult and most general aspects of the problem. Let us begin, instead, with the opposite end of the issue − namely, with cases of manifest injustice in which persons are treated in ways they do not deserve. An obvious example is that of a person punished for a crime he clearly did not commit; in this case, the punishment is deemed "unjust" because the person did not deserve to be punished. Now consider a running race in which the judges, for reasons of pure caprice, decided to award the first prize to the runner who came in fourth. We would say that the runner did not deserve the prize, whereas the fastest runner did. In the absence of any action by the other runners that would lead to their disqualification, the runner who finished the race first could be said to deserve the first prize; any allocation of prizes inconsistent with this would be unjust. The injustice would remain, whether the judges' decision to reallocate the prize was based on mere caprice or on a systematic preference for some irrelevant characteristic of the participants (such as beauty or racial origin).

What seems characteristic of all such cases is that the injustice springs from a violation of rules – rules that are legitimately expected to be applied by participants or affected parties. Such rules isolate certain considerations that are relevant to the outcome of the event and to the determination of rewards; such rules isolate other considerations that are either explicitly or presumptively *irrelevant*.

The concept of "desert" is violated when an irrelevant consideration is brought into the reckoning (for example, the plaintiff's preparedness to have sexual relations with the judge or the color of the runner's skin) or, no less important, when a relevant consideration is ignored (for example, who actually crossed the finish line first).

There is then a connection between the notion of justice and the existence of prevailing rules. The mere presence of rules is sufficient to establish the relevance of desert, and hence the possibility of just and unjust conduct by participants.

What seems crucial here is the legitimacy of the participants' expectations that the rules will be followed, whether those expectations are related to the behavior of officials and administrators within the system or to that of other participants. If these expectations truly are legitimate, then individuals who base their conduct on them do not deserve to have them disappointed. The basis of this argument is the observation that rules provide information as to how others, on whose actions one's well-being depends, will act. One commits oneself to particular actions on the basis of one's understanding of what others may or may not do. In doing so, one renders oneself vulnerable if others do not behave in the required way, and one will not *deserve* to be harmed, provided that one's expectations about others' conduct are legitimate. The crucial question, then, is, What makes expectations "legitimate"? We shall turn to this matter in the next section.

At this point, we should note simply that when rules do give rise to legitimate expectations, questions of justice necessarily obtrude. In this sense, rules imply the relevance of justice; and just conduct is, at least presumptively, conduct obedient to prevailing rules.

One implication of this argument is worth noting. Suppose, as we argued in Chapter 1, that rules have value because they provide information to each actor about the behavior of others and because they thereby allow each actor to pursue his goals in the light of reasonable expectations about what others will do. On this basis, if rules are administered unjustly or if individuals do not behave in accordance with rules (that is, if individuals behave unjustly in the sense outlined earlier), then rules no longer provide this information. Rules cease to accomplish that function for which they are valued. This argument provides an instrumental defense of justice. The ancient admonition, Let justice be done though the heavens fall, can be construed in this context as the demand that the rules be adhered to, come what may. Justice is valued because it involves independently valued adherence to rules. This rule-following interpretation of justice is quite different from the notion that particular rules are valued because they meet external standards of justice.

III.   Justice and promise keeping

So far we have argued that a person who violates a legitimate rule acts unjustly toward those who acted with the expectation that the rule would be followed. The question naturally arises as to what makes a rule, or the expectations a rule gives rise to, legitimate. Under what conditions, in other words, will violating a rule constitute unjust behavior? And what gives the notion of justice so defined moral force?

There are no surprises in our answer here. A rule is legitimate, and violations of it constitute unjust behavior, when the rule is the object of voluntary consent among participants in the rule-governed order. Why is this so? Because the provision of consent on a voluntary basis amounts to offering a *promise* to abide by the rules. Just conduct is conduct in accord with promises given. A person breaks a promise if he acts differently than, for morally proper reasons, those to whom the promise was made believe he will act. The morality of justice is, then, the morality of promise keeping. In this, we do no more than echo Thomas Hobbes:

. . . it is in the laws of the Commonwealth as in the laws of gaming: whatsoever the gamesters all agree on is injustice to none of them.[1]

---

[1] Thomas Hobbes, *Leviathan* (1651) (New York: Everyman Edition, 1943), part 2, ch. 30, p. 185.

From that law of nature . . . there followeth a third; which is this that men perform their covenants made: without which, covenants are in vain and but empty words, and . . . we are still in the condition of war. And in this law of nature consisteth the fountain and origin of *justice*. For where no covenant hath preceded . . . every man has right to everything, and consequently no action can be unjust. But when a covenant is made then to break it is unjust; and the definition of injustice is no other than the not performance of covenant. And whatsoever is not unjust is just.[2]

This formulation raises three questions, however. First, what is it that one's agreement commits one to do? Second, what are we to understand by "voluntary" agreement, and how does the requirement that the agreement be voluntary affect obligation? Third, how broadly can we interpret "agreement" or "consent" for the purposes of this argument? Let us deal with these questions in turn.

In response to the first, we offer only a minor clarification. When one freely agrees to the rules, one promises to do rather more than pursue what is best for oneself under the terms of the agreement. Specifically, although the rules will typically include instructions as to how violations are to be handled and what punishments are to attach to such violations, and although these instructions are therefore contained within the inclusive agreement, it seems wrongheaded to say that agreement implies only a willingness to accept the defined punishment for violations. Consent is to the *rules*, and the moral force of promise keeping is such that one is obligated to other players to play by those rules. To violate the rules may sometimes be personally profitable, but it will not be "just," and it will not become "just" simply by virtue of one's acceptance of punishment. "Just conduct" will consist in keeping one's promises to other players, that is, in abiding by agreed-on rules. A player, for example, who punches another with his fist in American football concedes a fifteen-yard penalty. But he also endures the moral opprobrium of having committed an "unjust" act, and it is expected that this purely moral dimension — the player's sense of justice — will carry weight in moderating his behavior.

It is important to make this point because, in some economists' discussions of the law, one obtains the impression that choosing whether to abide by the rules is like selecting a drink at a soft-drink machine; that is, one either abides by the rules and pays no penalty or fails to abide by the rules and simply pays the price of so doing, as reflected in the rules. But the legislated punishment is not to be construed simply as the "price" of an alternative course of action; it also symbolizes the fact that a "wrong" has been committed. Making a choice among alternative drinks is a morally neutral act; choosing between legitimate and illegi-

[2] Ibid., p. 74.

timate modes of behavior is not morally neutral (at least not if the legitimacy springs from the prior consent of the chooser).

The second question is related to the circumstances under which an agreement may be said to be genuinely voluntary. Clearly, a promise to abide by the rules that is obtained under duress is not binding in the way that a freely offered promise is binding. The victim of a holdup who promises to pay a million dollars from his bank account in exchange for his life does not fail to meet a totally legitimate expectation when he subsequently refuses to pay. In the same way, a starving man who agrees to run inordinate risks for a crust of bread cannot necessarily be held to be bound to the agreement, although he is presumably more bound than he would be had he refused, despite his adversity, to agree. In other words, the moral force of an obligation to keep a promise is blunted (but not necessarily eliminated) if the circumstances surrounding the giving of the promise involve nonvoluntary elements.

We must be careful here not to extend the argument too far. To say, for example, that the agreement is nonvoluntary if the bargaining strengths of the parties to it are not precisely equal seems absurdly restrictive. It seems that only in cases of extreme duress or outright coercion does agreement to the rules *not* morally bind the players. When A and B agree to marry, for example, we do not normally demand that their bargaining strengths or premarriage "threat strategies" or income positions or beauty or physical strength (or whatever each brings to the marriage) be equal (or even not unduly unequal) before the exchange of vows can be regarded as binding. We do not typically inquire whether A and B had other offers of marriage or could have had such offers. All that is required to give the "covenant" moral force is the absence of extreme duress. Indeed, even the presence of the paternal shotgun is not normally construed to remove the moral obligations entailed in the marriage entirely (and sometimes not to blunt those obligations at all).

It is worth making this point clearly so as to guard against the prospect of admitting alien concepts of "justice" through the back door under the cover of the "voluntariness" constraint. In some literature, the "justice" of abiding by an agreement is made entirely contingent on the justice of the status quo, the latter notion of "justice" usually making appeal to the relative income positions of the parties. We emphasize that the voluntariness of agreement is not to be so construed in our conception. It is only in those circumstances in which a promise would be held to be nonbinding (extracted by force or under conditions of total duplicity by one of the parties) that the requirements of justice, as we have defined it, would be waived.

The third general question raised by this conception of justice involves the issue of how broadly agreement or consent to the rules can be construed. Clearly, in most social contexts, players do not explicitly agree to the rules that apply to their interactions. Drivers do not, for example, construct the rules of the road by explicit consensus. How, then, can considerations of promise keeping be construed to apply in such cases? This question is central and long standing in any "social-contract" theory. Some scholars have sought to establish a presumptive obligation on the part of citizens to abide by the "rules" of a prevailing social order[3] on the basis of what "would have been agreed to."[4] To the extent that such obligations can be established, considerations of justice apply. For such purely *hypothetical* consent, however, the argument seems less than totally persuasive. It is not clear exactly how a person can be bound by promises he has not made, or how a person can be construed to have agreed to rules simply on the grounds that those rules can be presumed to make him better off.

Tacit, or *implicit*, consent, however, is another story. Tacit consent can be construed to be given to rules of a game by participants when they voluntarily participate. The mere fact of participation obligates each participant, as if by an explicit promise, to abide by the rules, provided that the participants have a genuine option not to participate if they so choose. Failure to abide by the rules would then be to treat other participants "unjustly." Participants' expectations that others will play by the rules become "legitimate" by virtue of the voluntariness of participation by all players. If, for example, a person asked to join an existing poker game and was permitted entry, he would seem to be no less obligated by considerations of justice to obey the rules than the other players, who had given explicit consent.

A similar point can be made with respect to another important group of "participants" in the social order — those who *administer* the rules. Again, we do not require the explicit agreement of judges, umpires, and enforcers on the structure of the rules in order to argue that these agents would be acting "unjustly" were they to violate or modify the rules in accordance with personal preferences. Those who administer a race presumably accept the rule that the first person across the finish line will win. Those who administer the legal system purport to be acting within the rules of that system. Those who enter the "game" in either case do so on the basis of an understanding of the rules, and in

---

[3] As is the object in Hobbes, *Leviathan*.

[4] As in the writing of John Rawls and others in the "justice as fairness" tradition. See John Rawls, *A Theory of Justice* (Cambridge, Mass.: Harvard University Press, 1971).

some sense the existence of rules amounts to an implicit promise made by administrators to all participants (actual and potential) that the rules will be administered faithfully.

If participation in a sporting event or parlor game − either as a player or as an administrator, judge, or enforcer − is sufficient to obligate all parties to abide by the rules, by virtue of considerations of justice can we not extrapolate such obligation to all social settings? Whether or not we can depends on whether individual participants in a given social order can be construed to be *voluntary* participants. For administrators of the rules and for those who voluntarily join (free immigrants, for example), the obligation seems clearly applicable. For general citizens, voluntariness of participation is not so clear. The problem is, of course, that participation amounts to playing the "only game in town." There may be no effective alternatives. Even in this case, however, there is some sense in which violation of the rules is "unjust" to other participants. Just what this sense is deserves some attention. Suppose that A, B, . . . , N are participants in a game the rules for which have been decided unilaterally by Z. Suppose, furthermore, that these rules have traditionally been observed − that A, B, . . . , N have played by them for some time. If A were now to inflict harm on B by breaking the rules, would we not say that B did not *deserve* to be harmed? Would not A's harming B be unjust in this sense? Would not B's *reasonable* expectation that A would continue to hold by the rules be a legitimate basis for B's conduct? Does not the mere fact that such rules have prevailed for a long time contribute to the legitimacy of B's expectations? If so, rules may be considered to be given tacit consent simply by virtue of their history or regular observance − even if there is no effective option to not playing and participation is involuntary in that sense. Of course, such tacit consent as a source of obligation to abide by existing rules does not imply quiescence toward efforts to change the rules. But this is a matter we shall discuss below.

Where does all this leave us with respect to the relation between rules and justice? It indicates that prevailing rules, simply by virtue of their existence, project an aura of justice. Behavior that contravenes prevailing rules amounts to unjust treatment of other participants in the social arena, because the others have legitimate expectations that all persons will behave in accordance with the rules. The legitimacy, not the reasonableness, of the expectations is crucial, and this legitimacy arises because, and to the extent that, participation in the activities governed by the rules is, or can be construed to be, voluntary. Voluntary participation amounts to agreement to the rules. It constitutes a tacit promise to abide by prevailing rules, and the breaking of such a promise is equivalent to unjust conduct because it involves treating others in ways in which they do not deserve to be treated.

IV. Justice among rules

Although the discussion of just conduct set out in the preceding two sections has some affinities with notions in contemporary social philosophy, it is not the most common approach to "justice." Typically, justice is introduced as a criterion for *evaluating* alternative rules or institutions. This criterial usage of justice characterizes many strands of normative political and social theory — from natural law to modern theses advancing the norms for "distributive" and "social" justice.[5] It is, in this sense, much more common to think of justice constraining rules than to think of rules constraining justice.

In this section, we advance the proposition that the business of deciding what rules are just — that is, of deriving a meaning for justice as a criterion of choice among rules — is a particular instance of decision making within prevailing rules. Such an argument requires the recognition that the decision as to what the rules shall be is itself made in the context of more abstract rules that apply to the choice among rules. We shall call rules at this more abstract level *meta-rules*. Then it follows from our earlier discussion that rules are just if agreed-on meta-rules dictating their selection have been observed.

Although this is an entirely natural extension of the Hobbesian position, we here part company with Hobbes, at least in the strict sense of Hobbes's exposition. In Hobbes's view, the notion of an "unjust law" is meaningless. "No law," he claims, "can be unjust. The law is made by the sovereign power and all that is done by such power is warranted and owned by everyone of the people; and that which every man will have so, no man can say is unjust."[6] But as Hobbes's discussion makes clear, all this is contingent on individuals' agreement on the principle of sovereign authority. It is the more abstract agreement on the structure of civil order that makes the law derived under that structure "just." And so it is for us — for the essence of the constitutionalist approach is that political action (including the making of laws) be conducted according to certain rules (or meta-rules). A "just law" is then a meaningful concept; it is one that is derived under agreed-on institutions or, equivalently, one that does not violate agreed-on rules under which those institutions operate.

[5] We discuss distributive justice in constitutional perspective in Chapter 8.
[6] Hobbes, *Leviathan*, part 2, ch. 30, p. 185.

It is important to recognize that we are here weakening the requirements for just *conduct*. Hitherto, conduct was described as just if it did not violate agreed-on rules related to that conduct. Now, conduct is also considered to be just if it does not violate just rules (defined as rules emerging under agreed-on meta-rules). Since the meta-rules in question may not *require* agreement on rules directly, an "agreed-on rule" and a "just rule" are distinct concepts. We may not require a rule to be agreed on for it to be binding, provided that the rule in question emerged under agreed-on meta-rules.

The distinction between agreed-on rules and just rules — the recognition that agreement can be applied at different levels of abstraction — somewhat complicates the discussion of the requirements of justice. This is an issue we shall attempt to clarify in Section V. At this point, we shall address a different issue, which is related to the connection between abstraction and voluntariness. That is, since justice within rules is contingent on the rules having been *voluntarily* agreed to, we must make some sense of the notion of voluntary agreement at the more abstract, meta-rule level. What does it mean to refer to a meta-rule as the subject of voluntary consent? What, for example, would involuntary consent involve at that meta-rule level?

In fact, the shift to more and more abstract levels of discourse serves to modify concern about the voluntariness of agreement — at least in one major sense. One can, of course, in principle imagine direct physical coercion being applied by one agent to others at the meta-level. But one has to ask whether the application of force is at all likely. At the extreme level, where the thick Rawlsian veil of ignorance is drawn and individuals are totally uncertain as to their future positions, individuals have no interests to defend. Any reason that any one of them has for preferring one set of rules over another will be a reason for all others to prefer that set of rules as well. In what sense would, or could, any individual find reason to coerce others?

Moreover, we must bear in mind that the agents at this abstract level *wish* to secure agreements voluntarily, and for good reason: It is the capacity of such voluntary agreements to establish moral obligations that drives the whole "constitutional exercise." Agents desire a stable institutional order so that they will have an appropriate context in which to pursue their (imagined) future life plans. If a *forced* agreement will not serve to legitimate the rules, it will not establish a moral obligation to abide by the rules; so forceful extraction of agreement has no point.

Furthermore, reference to extreme need, and more general concerns about relative positions in the constitutional status quo that might be taken to offend the "voluntariness" requirement, also seems irrelevant at this most abstract level. If individuals are totally ignorant as to their future positions, they have no separately identifiable interests; there is a fundamental equality of position. It seems impossible that agreements reached in such a context could reflect unacceptable differences in status quo positions. Accordingly, however exactly one might wish to express the requirements for voluntariness in agreements reached, all such requirements appear to be met to an increasing extent as one moves to higher and higher levels of abstraction in the rule formation exercise. This fact represents a possible major justification for the whole "constitutionalist" approach.

V. Just rules, agreed rules, and just conduct

The central argument in the previous section was that justice among rules is simply a case of justice within rules once removed. By implication, justice among meta-rules is a matter of justice within meta-meta-rules, and so on. In this sense, justice within rules becomes the paradigmatic case. Any appeal to considerations of justice in an interaction is an appeal to agreements made with respect to that interaction or to agreements made with respect to the rules under which that interaction takes place.

This line of reasoning requires us to clarify the distinction between rules that are "just" in the sense defined (that is, rules that emerge from voluntarily agreed-on procedures for determining rules) and rules that are agreed on. We must also point out that our paradigmatic notion of just conduct, or justice within the rules, entails an extension of our definition of just conduct to include conduct that is obedient both to agreed-on rules and to just rules, as defined.

To amplify what is at stake here, we shall offer a simple example. A tennis match of some significance is in its fifth and final set. Individual A is leading 5−4, and B is to serve. Suddenly, the umpire announces a change in the rules: The net is to be raised one foot. Could not B legitimately complain that this rule change is "unjust," that he does not deserve to be treated in this way? or that A does not deserve an unanticipated advantage? Following the reasoning set out in the previous two sections, it would indeed seem that A and B are being treated unjustly. The rules to which they tacitly agreed when they decided to participate have been changed. They have not implicitly promised to obey the new rule, so they cannot be accused of unjust behavior if they violate it. On the contrary, the rule to which A implicitly agreed has been violated in A's favor: B has been treated unjustly.

Yet such a conclusion may well be premature. We must ask whether the rule change in question has been made in accordance with the recognized meta-rules. Suppose, for example, that a properly constituted body, say, the World Tennis Federation, has decided to raise the net in the game of tennis by appropriate adherence to its own rules of procedure. To take the simplest case, suppose that the decision is made some time in advance and is to take effect at midnight on New Year's Eve, 1985, and that the match between A and B is the final of the 1985 Australian Tennis Championship, held under World Tennis Association rules and occurring on New Year's Eve. The match has taken rather longer than expected, and at 4 − 5 in the fifth set with B to serve, midnight strikes. In this case, since A and B were aware of the prospective rule change and the possibility that the match would last until midnight, both A and B can reasonably be held to be bound by the new rules.

If, however, the World Tennis Federation did not announce the rule change in advance and the umpire was simply notified by cable of the rule change at midnight, then neither A nor B could be construed to be bound by the new rule by virtue of direct implicit agreement. But if the federation's actions were procedurally "just" − that is, obedient to agreed-on meta-rules governing its behavior in determining the rules − then the rule change would not be a violation of justice. The prevailing meta-rules would have been faithfully applied. The point here is that A and B are to be seen as tacitly accepting not just the rules of the game but also the meta-rules − indeed, a whole sequence of rules of various degrees of abstraction. The mere existence of such meta-rules testifies to the prospect that rules may be changed, and any change obedient to these meta-rules is presumptively just. The prospect of rule change is something that players agree to face, much like changes in the weather. Unlike changes in the weather, however, rule changes are the result of human activity and hence come under the scrutiny of "justice." The question at issue is whether rule makers, in changing the rules, violate *legitimate* expectations, and the answer is that they do not, provided that they follow the relevant meta-rules. The requirement that no rule change ever occur is one possible meta-rule, but if it is not the prevailing meta-rule a blind following of the meta-rule forbidding rule change would be *unjust*. If, for example, the umpire refused to alter the height of the net, in spite of a clear specification in the meta-rules that he do so, B would receive an undeserved advantage and A would lose an advantage he did not deserve to lose.

This is a matter of some account in political−economic contexts.

Consider the case in which government action creates change in the income of a specified group by means of some regulation restricting entry into a particular industry. Now suppose that after a time government removes such protective regulation. Individuals will lose income, and the individuals who lose will not necessarily be those who gained in the first place. Those who purchase New York taxi medallions and stand to lose if the number of medallions is increased are not necessarily those who benefited from the introduction of medallions. The case is sometimes made in this connection that the government action is "unjust," either in removing the regulation or perhaps in introducing the regulation in the first place. Similarly, the charge is occasionally made that when governments do pay compensation to the victims of policy changes, such action is unjust to taxpayers who must foot the bill.

In the justice within rules perspective, however, none of these claims is necessarily valid. Provided that government action in each case is itself obedient to the prevailing and accepted rules governing public-sector conduct, there is no violation of precepts of justice. As a matter of fact, modern political arrangements seem to be such that those who allocate public revenues can allocate them more or less as they choose or as political considerations suggest, in which case, the government simply cannot in such contexts violate principles of justice. To argue that government action is unjust is to claim that it violates agreed-on rules of public conduct. That is simply the way arguments about justice must properly proceed.

Now, it may be that the rules are unclear, as they often are in social contexts. There is some question, for example, as to whether regulation may in some situations amount to a "taking" and hence violate existing constitutional rules. There is also some question as to whether judicial interpretation may, in some cases, amount to a change in the rules and, in this sense, raise the issue of what role the courts properly exercise in the whole institutional order. Furthermore, certain rules may overlap with others at the same level of abstraction and indicate rather different behavioral restrictions. In all such cases, justice requires clarification of the rules and reconciliation of ambiguities. One major clarification along these lines involves the recognition of the level of abstraction at which agreement is to be applied. But the *grammar* of arguments about justice at least seems clear.

One other possible ambiguity should be addressed. What are we to make of the status of agreements made outside the structure of rules? Clearly, when the set of individuals party to the agreement includes all the individuals who compose the political order, such agreements cannot conceivably violate precepts of justice. But when these sets of people are different, such agreements may be unjust. That is to say, the agreed-on rule structure may preclude certain sorts of agreements.

It is important to make this point in order to clarify the status of simple two-person market exchange in our conception. The parties to that exchange agree voluntarily to its terms. If one party subsequently fails to live up to those terms, he is presumptively acting unjustly toward the other party. But this presumption of unjust conduct can only be that — for it may be that the more inclusive set of constitutional rules explicitly precludes small-number voluntary transactions of various sorts or otherwise establishes obligations that conflict with those imposed in small-number transactions. Consider, for example, the case in which the firms in an industry form a cartel by means of an agreement, voluntarily entered into, the object of which is to restrict entry into the industry, reduce output, and raise prices. Suppose, now, that one of the parties to that agreement reneges on the terms, cuts prices, and makes substantial profits at the other firms' expense. Is that cartel breaker acting "unjustly" with respect to other firms in the industry? Surely yes. Yet in doing so, the firm is also ceasing to act unjustly with respect to consumers of the firm's product, if the more inclusive set of constitutional rules constrains restrictions on cartel deals. Considerations of justice here conflict, precisely as they would if A made separate agreements with B and C that for unexpected reasons turned out to be in conflict. But whereas in the case of ordinary agreements that conflict, considerations of justice do not indicate which agreement should be decisive, there is a distinct presumption in the cartel case that the constitutional rules should be decisive. In this sense, some amplification of Hobbes's characterization is in order. Although it remains true that "whatsoever the gamesters all agree on is injustice to none of *them*" (emphasis added), this does not rule out the possibility that the gamesters are acting "unjustly" in a more global sense. Whether or not that is so will depend, however, on the same basic principle — namely, whether the gamesters have prior, more inclusive agreements with other agents that are, or ought to be, overriding.

VI.   Conclusions

In this chapter, our aim has been to offer an account of the nature of justice that spills naturally out of our constitutionalist–contractarian perspective. We have specifically defined justice in terms of conduct that does not violate agreed-on rules. One major implication of this approach is that justice is not a "primary" concept. Rather, it is derived from two logically prior notions: first, that agreements carry moral obligations to abide by the terms of those agreements; and second, that appeals to justice take place within an institutional context that serves to assign justice its meaning.

The approach also suggests a grammar of "justice" arguments. In particular, appeals to justice are appeals to matters of fact, as well as value. What are the rules that govern particular areas of conduct? Were those rules agreed to, or can they be construed to have been agreed to? These are questions of fact. There remains, of course, the value question of the extent to which agreements should bind the agreers. But this issue cannot, as a general matter of principle, be decided by considerations of justice. Justice becomes relevant only when the force of voluntary agreement is taken as given.

We should finally emphasize the restrictive purpose of this chapter. Our central aim has been to relate the notion of justice to the rules of social order. The nature of the argument, however, has made it necessary to skirt perilously close to areas of deep philosophical inquiry for which our own claims to competence are, at best, marginal. We should therefore make clear the absence of any putative claim to have made a positive contribution to the analysis of justice itself.

The central point is important, however, to the overall thrust of our argument and, in our view, to a proper understanding of the concept of justice. Any discussion of justice, whether by learned philosophers or common people, takes for granted that the interaction of persons in society occurs within a structure of rules. Appeals to the considerations of justice are appeals to those rules. In this sense, once justice is deemed a desirable attribute of conduct or of social order, there is established an indirect "reason of rules" – and an independent demand for a constitutionalist or rule-focused perspective on social life.

CHAPTER 8

Politics without rules, II: Distributive justice and distributive politics

I.   Introduction

In Chapter 7 we discussed the connection between rules and justice. We argued that a meaningful discussion of justice presupposes the existence of rules and that a just outcome emerges when the relevant rules have been followed.

Such a view of justice is not common, in either economic or broader circles. Orthodox conceptions of justice invoke the notion of distributive justice, or "equity." In this view, the justice or injustice of an outcome is held to be an intrinsic property of the outcome itself and to be context independent. To determine whether one social outcome is more "just" than another, one need merely investigate the relative positions of individuals in each. Relative positions are typically measured by reference to individuals' incomes or wealth, although sometimes consumption of, or access to, certain "crucial" consumption items (e.g., health, housing, food, or education) can be regarded as a superior basis for comparison.

It is not our objective here to criticize this familiar conception of distributive justice; in what follows, we shall take the normative relevance of "equality," or "less inequality," somehow construed, as given. Our concern is, rather, to examine the concept of distributive justice from the constitutional perspective. Our task is to ask, given the normative judgment that equality is desirable, what set of institutional arrangements are likely to be most conducive to securing that "equality" (or "less inequality"). Are there any reasons for believing that the political order will generate a more nearly equal distribution of income than a free market would generate (as seems to be commonly assumed)? What "rules" of political order are likely to generate more "equitable" outcomes?

Before we address these issues, however, it is important to recognize that in posing them we adopt a perspective on distributive justice very different from the orthodox one. We shall therefore begin our discussion by attempting to characterize the orthodox approach and by showing how the constitutional view raises additional, crucial issues.

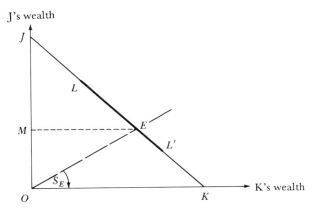

Figure 8.1

We shall also indicate what is, in our judgment, analytically incoherent about the orthodox conception.

II.   Distributive justice: the conventional view

Characterizing the normal conception of distributive justice involves posing and attempting to answer the question, How should total product be distributed? All possible distributions of some aggregate are considered, and some criteria are used to select the "best." A common analogy is the division of a pie among contending children, each of whom is presumed to want more pie. Consider, for example, a simple two-person community, composed of persons J and K. In terms of simple geometry, the set of possible distributions is given by the line *JK* in Figure 8.1. Niggardly nature presents the community with an aggregate *OJ* (equal to *OK*), which can be given all to J (at point *J*) or all to K (at point *K*), respectively, or distributed between J and K in various proportions. We represent the distribution as the ratio of J's share to K's share; at *E*, for example, we can depict this ratio as the slope of the ray from the origin to *E*, S_E. Alternative measures of the distribution might be the difference between S_E and unity (i.e., equality), or the variance of levels or the amount assigned to the poorer individual (at *E*, *OM*) or something more complex. It is normally more or less presumed that, ceteris paribus, equality is best. In this abstract characterization it is perhaps difficult to justify anything other than equality (though it may not be a trivial matter to justify equality either).

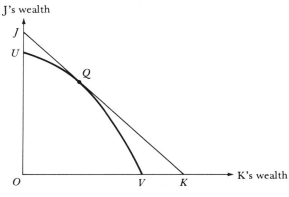

Figure 8.2

Economists and others typically argue that this characterization is inadequate in two significant respects. First, the pie does not present itself as an aggregate. Rather, it comes already sliced, the size of the slices being determined by the relative productive capacities of individuals. That is, there is a point on the *JK* line (let it be *Q* in Figure 8.2) that represents a sort of status quo point from which *re*distribution via some means must occur. Second, as redistribution occurs, the size of the pie changes. The general presumption is that as we move away from *Q*, the pie shrinks at an accelerating rate as "excess burden" arises on both the tax and the transfer side of the redistributive process. Accordingly, the relevant possibilities frontier becomes something like *UV* in Figure 8.2: Only points on *UV* are feasible; points on *JK* other than *Q* are not. Armed with this concession to reality, the normative analysis becomes one of "trading off" pie size against pie distribution, and the famous "equity–efficiency" conflict emerges. The "policy problem," then, presents itself in two dimensions: first, that of organizing the operation of policy instruments so that the cost in terms of pie forgone in achieving the ideal distribution is minimized; and second, that of determining how much distributive justice should be sacrificed in order to keep the pie as large as possible.

III.   The constitutional perspective and institutional incidence

There are several things wrong with this typical characterization of distributive justice. Consider first the conceptual philosophical issues. As a way of reflecting abstractly on one's distributive objectives – as a way of giving content to the notion of distributive justice — the conjectural model is perhaps innocent enough. It seems natural to pose the question, "If I were assigned the task of dividing the pie, what should I do?" But this question presupposes that questions of distributive justice do, in fact, present themselves this way. It suggests that distributions are *chosen* by some single agent, or by some decision rule.

But distributions are not chosen. Social outcomes, with their distributional characteristics "built in," *emerge* from a complex interaction of individual agents, each pursuing his own ends and each connected to others under a set of prevailing rules. Of course, it is conceivable that the prevailing rules could be such that outcomes (or specific distributions) would be chosen by a single agent. Totally despotic orders are not unknown. Is this the implicit model of politics that moral and social philosophers presume in dealing with questions of distributive justice? This model of politics does, indeed, seem to be what economists have in mind when they carry abstract philosophizing to the "relevant" policy level. But if the distribution is chosen by a despot, the model of Figure 8.1 is entirely inadequate. The relevant social setting will now involve *three* persons, not two. In addition to J and K, who are claimants on the aggregate pie, there is H, who is to do the cutting and allocating. If we model H as we do J and K, treating all as having conflicting demands for pie, then H will appropriate the entire pie for himself. If, on the other hand, we presume H to have altruistic concern for J and K, then, on the assumption of behavioral symmetry, we must model J and K likewise. The set of feasible distributions in Figure 8.1 is reduced from JK to LL', since distributions outside those limits will involve voluntary transfer between the parties to secure L and L'. In the same way H can be presumed to transfer to J and K up to the limits of his charitable impulses, just as if all the output had accrued to H in the first place. In other words, any conceptualization of the distributive-justice problem in terms of the unilateral choice of a distributive outcome effectively presupposes that the status quo distribution is one in which the chooser owns everything. This manner of setting up the problem virtually guarantees that distributive justice will be infeasible. Moreover, any minimal-state, free-market distribution such as Q in Figure 8.2 seems certain to be more equitable than that required to make redistribution possible. Considerations of distributive justice would, therefore, seem to argue persuasively in favor of rules that would deny the power to transfer to political institutions altogether.

The immediate response to this criticism is, of course, that the despot model is not presupposed. Assigning political agents the power to make transfers is not the same as assigning them an unqualified right to the use of the revenue from which transfers are to be made. Political agents cannot simply make transfers to themselves. But if this is so, we must ask why. We must, in other words, trace *how* political agents are constrained in the distribution of the pie. And the relevant constraints here are not the familiar "economic" ones having to do with how the size of the pie changes when the level of public transfer activity increases. The relevant constraints are those embodied in the *rules of the political game* that shape the magnitude and pattern of transfers. To put the point more generally, different institutional arrangements, ranging from those embodied in some Nozickean "minimal state" to those characterized by the modern welfare state, where explicit restrictions on the power to transfer are absent, will generate different patterns of distributive outcomes. The problem of practical politics is to choose a feasible institutional arrangement that will generate a distributional pattern most congruent with the requirements of distributive justice.

The central point here is a familiar one in the context of efficiency analysis. So-called market failure problems (attributable to public goods, generalized externalities, and monopoly elements in private goods supply), although sufficient to indicate the presence of unrealized gains from exchange, are now widely recognized as constituting an inadequate normative case for government intervention in market processes. There is no necessary presumption that simply because markets are imperfect, political processes will work better. On the contrary, as public-choice theory reminds us, there are very good reasons for doubting the capacity of political processes to achieve Pareto optimality. The normatively relevant comparison is between two imperfect institutions. The mere observation that one institution or the other is imperfect − that markets "fail" − is simply not sufficient to establish a case for government "intervention." So much is accepted, at least in principle, although the point seems to require continual reiteration.

In the realization of distributive justice, however, there is a precisely analogous point, though it seems hardly to have been noted. The point is this: It is not enough to lament the distribution that emerges from − or is *presumed* to emerge from[1] − a freely operating market. One must

---

[1] Presumption is all that is possible in economies where the public sector absorbs one-third to one-half of total product and where unmeasured effects of collective activity via regulation ripple throughout the economy and influence the income distribution in untold ways.

show that the effect of the political process on the distribution is in the direction of equality. Or, to put the question most starkly, is movement toward equality institutionally feasible? It is ironic that despite the extensive literature on distributional policy, this basic question is almost never posed, let alone answered.[2] The virtue of the constitutional perspective is that it places this question firmly at center stage. It does so by shifting the domain of normative inquiry from the set of imaginable *income distributions* to the set of feasible *institutional arrangements* from which income distributions will emerge.

What seems to us necessary here is a set of "institutional incidence exercises." Consider, for example, a familiar tax incidence exercise in orthodox public finance. Suppose that the "policy maker" is conceived to have access to several taxes: an excise on beer, a land tax, and a corporate profits tax. In the conventional setting, we might, for example, ask, What are the distributional consequences of imposing the beer tax rather than an equirevenue land tax? We trace the distributional implications of this tax substitution in terms of the "burdens borne" by various groups (consumers of beer, specific factors in the beer industry, etc.) and burdens reduced for others. Only then is it possible to apply the normative criteria of distributive justice to decide whether the tax substitution is desirable and what mixture of tax instruments is "best." With the tax instruments available, only certain distributions are feasible and none of them may correspond to the ideal. As we have emphasized, this approach is inadequate because it ignores the fact that any such tax choice emerges out of a political process in which "distributive justice" will be secured only if it serves the interests of those who are decisive in the political game. The approach, however, does recognize that not all distributions are feasible and that the distributional implications of alternative policy instruments must be traced before any normative recommendations can be offered. There is, at least, the recognition that alternative taxes rather than alternative distributions are the objects of normative evaluation. Here, we extend that recognition to a more appropriate level of discourse. Rather than focusing on the distributional implications of alternative *taxes*, we focus instead on the distributional implications of alternative *sets of rules*. In that sense, our concern is with the "incidence" of alternative institutions.

---

[2] For a notable exception, see Dan Usher *The Economic Prerequisite to Democracy* (Oxford: Basil Blackwell, 1981).

IV.   The incidence of unrestricted majoritarianism

In this and the ensuing sections, we shall attempt to derive the pattern of distributional outcomes that can be expected to emerge under majority rule, subject to a variety of institutional restrictions.[3] Our object in doing this is to take political institutions more or less as we know them and ask, first, whether there is any theoretical presumption that political processes tend to generate greater "distributive justice" than, say, a predominantly market-oriented regime; and second, what restrictions on the operation of political institutions seem likely to be conducive to the pursuit of "distributive justice." Throughout, we shall deal with an extremely simple, highly abstract model of majority rule.

Specifically, we shall consider a simple three-person community, composed of persons A, B, and C.[4] All three vote, and all are assumed to cast their votes in accordance with their interests.[5] There is no altruism; all aim to maximize their own real incomes.[6] We define the length of a period to be the length of time between elections, so there is by definition one election each period. Finally, in order to focus solely on the distributional consequences of majority rule, we assume that the only thing government does is make transfers; that is, we abstract from any provision of public goods that the government may undertake.[7] Because we wish to focus on the distributions that emerge, we shall depict all outcomes as a triplet of the form [a, b, c], where a is the total income of A, b the total income of B, and c the total income of C.

Consider, on this basis, the conceptual benchmark represented by the distribution under an entirely "free" market order. No transfers, either public or private, occur. This distribution will reflect individuals'

---

[3] For a very general examination of some of the redistributional implications of majority rule, see James M. Buchanan, "The Political Economy of Franchise in the Welfare State," in *Capitalism and Freedom: Problems and Prospects*, ed. Richard T. Selden (Charlottesville: University Press of Virginia, 1975), pp. 52–77.

[4] These "persons" can be conceived as standing for completely homogeneous groups of equal size.

[5] This assumption is by no means unexceptionable, as we have argued elsewhere. See Geoffrey Brennan and James Buchanan, "The Logic of the Levers" (Center for Study of Public Choice, Fairfax, Va., 1983, mimeographed). It does, however, follow conventional public-choice practice and is highly convenient here.

[6] In Chapter 4, we attempted to justify this assumption as an analytically appropriate tool.

[7] This assumption is a "fudge." A market order requires institutions to protect property rights and enforce contracts, and such institutions require access to resources in order to function. Taxes will then not be zero in the absence of transfers. However, it is useful to assume that there are no taxes in the zero-transfer case.

differing productive capacities, preparedness to take risks, propensities to accumulate, and differing histories. Therefore, we would not expect this outcome to reflect distributional equality, in general. We denote this "free-market outcome" by the vector $\mathbf{M} = [m_a, m_b, m_c]$, where m_i is the ith individual's market income. Without loss of generality, let A be the richest and C the poorest, so that $m_a > m_b > m_c$. The total of the m's is national income more or less as conventionally measured.

Let us now introduce the prospect of governmental transfer, assuming that majority rule is the only operative constraint. As a point of departure, consider the case in which all transfers are "lump sum," that is, total income can be redistributed at will without loss. Aggregate money income (and the aggregate wealth stock) are totally unaffected by the transfer process. On this basis, suppose initially that B and C form a decisive coalition. Then, clearly, they will rationally take all of A's income (and wealth). To do otherwise would be to forgo income that the majority could costlessly appropriate and would prefer to have. The outcome will then be of the form $\mathbf{L} = [0, l_b, l_c]$, where $l_b + l_c = Y_M$. Note that no such outcome is stable. Outcome $\mathbf{L}$ can be defeated at the next election by a coalition between, say, A and B involving an outcome of the form $\mathbf{J} = [j_a, j_b, 0]$, where $j_b, > l_b$, and $j_a + j_b = Y_M$; or alternatively by a coalition between A and C involving an outcome of the form $\mathbf{K} = [k_a, 0, k_c]$, where $k_c > l_c$ and $k_a + k_c = Y_M$. Some such coalition in which two of the three parties are made better off must always exist. The situation here is the familiar one in public-choice theory (and in game theory) in which every possible outcome can be defeated under majority rule by some other. *No* outcome is inherently stable. Rather, we would expect continuous "cycling" as the composition of the decisive majority coalition changed. Nevertheless, whatever the precise identity of the majority coalition, all outcomes here will exhibit the same characteristic feature: the income of the minority member will always be driven to zero. Transfers will always be pushed to the confiscatory level.

We should note that parties to a prevailing majority coalition have an incentive to form binding agreements to maintain the coalition, for by entering such an agreement each majority member avoids a fifty–fifty chance of receiving a zero income in the *next* period. Of course, it would not be rational to refuse unilaterally to break the coalition. One could then lose only if one's current partner decided to break the agreement. Despite the continuous pressure for a coalition to break down, however, the possibility that a particular minority will be exploited systematically over a long sequence of electoral periods cannot be ruled out.

Three general points should be noted about this simple model. First, given the assumption that all transfers are lump sum, it is clear that the "benchmark" pretax, pretransfer income distribution is of no significance at all. Each individual has an expected average income over any sequence of electoral periods of $\frac{1}{3} Y_M$. No one is intrinsically "richer" than anyone else. Differential labor productivities or differential propensities to save or take risks exercise no influence at all on the distributional outcome, not even as some relevant point of departure. No one can properly be said to "own" anything, except what he can extract from the political process itself. And what the individual does extract is his only for the duration of the current electoral period. Here, the simple pie-carving analogy is perfectly proper. There *is* a fixed pie, and it *is* up for grabs.

Second, because the precise composition of the decisive majority at each point is unpredictable, each individual naturally has the same expected income over any future electoral sequence, namely $\frac{1}{3} Y_M$. In itself, this equalization of expected incomes can be interpreted as a major step toward distributive justice, as normally construed. The equality of *expected* income, however, has to be evaluated in light of the fact that there will be, at any point in the electoral sequence, one party that has zero income. Moreover, there is the possibility that particular coalitions may turn out to be stable over many elections, in which event the same party will face totally confiscatory transfer policy for substantial periods. Given this fact, the failure of standard criteria of distributive justice to address distributions of *fluctuating* parameters seems a major inadequacy. The impact of majoritarian political process on distributive justice in this simple model remains rather unclear.

Third, the assumption of lump-sum transfers is highly unrealistic. The *level* of income generated under the majoritarian system will necessarily be reduced by the revolving ownership rights. Consider, for example, the incentives for A, currently a party to the majority coalition, to accumulate capital assets when he recognizes that there is at least a one-in-three chance that he will be the exploited minority in the next election and have his assets confiscated. Incentives to acquire skills that add to labor income, to take risks, or to pursue entrepreneurial opportunities are substantially muted by the fact that the individual expects to reap only a fraction of the attendant benefits. Furthermore, securing membership in the majority coalition is a privately profitable activity. If, as seems likely, the time and energy individuals devote to becoming part of the decisive coalition have positive value when used in alternative ways, the expenditure of such time and energy is a net loss to the community. Such losses fall under the rubric of "rent-seeking" losses and are being increasingly recognized as major sources of inefficiency in contexts where institutional structures create opportunities for private gain that do not involve increased production.[8]

All this implies that transfers can be "lump sum" only in a very narrow sense. It may, in any period, be profitable for the prevailing majority to confiscate all the minority's income and assets, but in making plans for future electoral periods, all agents can be expected to bear in mind the prospect that they themselves will be minority members and that their assets will be confiscated. Therefore, there will be much less available for confiscation than there otherwise would be. In particular, the sum of post–tax-transfer incomes will be significantly less than Y_M at all points in the electoral sequence.

In light of this fact, all may well be better off in the expected sense if restrictions are placed on taxes and transfers in order to limit redistribution from the minority to the majority at any point. Moreover, such restrictions would have a presumptively desirable distributional consequence in that the distribution would be less inequitable at each point in the electoral sequence. We shall therefore turn, in Section V, to a brief examination of various possible restrictions that might be imposed on the tax-transfer process.

V. Tax rules and distribution under majority rule

Retaining the basic model of majority rule set out in the previous section, we shall proceed to examine the nature of distributional outcomes that emerge from political process in the presence of fiscal restrictions of various types, assuming that tax-transfer operations generate "excess burdens" and generalized efficiency losses for the community. We shall consider, in turn, restrictions imposed on the taxing process and the transfer process, adding an additional restriction at each turn. First, we shall suppose that the constitution restricts the taxing authorities to a single-rate income tax, no other restrictions being applied. Then we shall add the requirement that the income tax be levied at a uniform proportional rate on *all* individuals. We shall add the further restriction that transfers be paid in equal per capita

---

[8] For extended treatments of this phenomenon, see James Buchanan, Robert Tollison, and Gordon Tullock (eds.), *Toward a Theory of the Rent-Seeking Society* (College Station: Texas A & M University Press, 1980).

amounts, in the form of a "demogrant." Finally, we shall consider a direct *constitutional* selection of the tax-rate−transfer level.

1. Flat-rate income tax

Suppose that the majority is restricted to the use of a flat-rate tax on money income in imposing taxes on the minority. That is, although only minority members pay the tax, there is a well-defined tax base, money income, and a single rate applied equally to all minority group members. The significance of this restriction is twofold. First, the single-rate restriction is important because it prevents the majority from levying a tax that discriminates over inframarginal units of the minority members' money income. Just as a discriminating monopolist can charge higher prices on inframarginal units of product and thereby secure some of the value of the consumer surplus otherwise accruing to the purchaser, so a taxing authority can appropriate some (and in the limit all) of the citizens' consumer surplus by means of an *appropriately regressive* tax.[9] The requirement of a uniform tax rate across all units of an individual's income rules out any such prospects.

Second, the requirement that taxes be levied on money *income* explicitly rules out the power of the majority to confiscate the minority's asset holdings − something that would be feasible under a wealth tax, for example. Income from assets can be taxed at the same rate as income from other sources, but the assets themselves remain more or less inviolable.[10]

Several things follow from these restrictions on the tax side. First, there will be, for each individual, a maximum amount of revenue, R_i^*, that can be obtained from him through the flat-rate income tax. Second, there will be for each individual an associated minimal income level, n_i, which he secures, post-tax, when faced with the maximum revenue tax rate. Third, we know that the taxing process will inflict net losses on taxpayers, over and above the revenue collected, as individuals are induced by the tax to substitute tax-free leisure for income.

---

[9] See Geoffrey Brennan and James Buchanan, *The Power to Tax* (Cambridge University Press, 1980), ch. 3, for a detailed exposition of this point.

[10] Under inadequate indexing provisions, inflation makes it possible for taxing authorities to appropriate part of the real value of the assets themselves (by driving the net-of-tax real rate of return below zero). Here, we assume that monetary authorities are constitutionally restricted from engineering inflation for redistributive purposes, or at least are independent of in-period political pressures. See Brennan and Buchanan, *Power to Tax*, chs. 5 and 6.

These claims can be readily justified analytically,[11] but it is perhaps necessary here only to provide an analogy. We can think of the majority as owning a monopoly right in the sale of the minority's factor services. The maximum tax revenue obtainable corresponds to the maximum monopoly profit from the sale of those services, and the minority's minimal income can be thought of as the cost borne by the monopolist of providing those services and accruing to the basic productive factors (in this case, the minority). The excess burden is then analogous to the efficiency losses associated with monopoly.

On this basis, it is clear that the decisive majority will always apply the revenue-maximizing tax rate to the minority's income. To do otherwise would be to forgo transfers that the majority coalition could obtain. This will not, however, drive the minority's net money income to zero; tax rates will necessarily fall short of 100 percent. To apply a tax rate in excess of the revenue-maximizing rate will, by definition, reduce the revenues available for transfer to the majority. At the same time, the majority will never willingly impose taxes on itself, because taxes involve an excess burden. Even if the revenue were to be returned to the taxpayer group in lump-sum form, the group would still receive less than would be required to compensate for the imposition of the tax.

Consider, for example, the case where A is in the minority, and B and C are in the majority. Then A will face the revenue-maximizing tax rate and receive a net total income of n_a, whereas B and C will pay no taxes and will receive R_a^* to divide between them in some proportion. That is, the resultant outcome will be $J_A = [n_a, m_b + S_b, m_c + S_c]$, where $S_b + S_c = R_a^*$. Analogously, when B is the minority, the outcome will be $J_B = [m_a + S_a', n_b, m_c + S_c']$, where $S_a' + S_c' = R_b^*$. The result would be equivalent if C were the minority.

As in the case of unrestricted majoritarianism, we cannot predict which majority coalition will prevail. No outcome exists that cannot be defeated under majority rule. "Cycling" can be expected, as the identity of the decisive coalition continuously shifts. Such cycling is here bounded, however, in the sense that no one's income can be reduced to a level below n_i. Obversely, the best that any group can conceivably do is to receive maximum revenue from *both* of the other groups. This is, of course, unlikely, but a majority member may have to consent to be taxed in order to provide sufficient revenue to bribe another group to join the majority coalition. Suppose, for example, that J_A prevails and that the maximum revenue R_a^* is split equally between B and C. Then A will seek to form a coalition that is best for himself. If there is more

---

[11] See, for example, ibid., chs. 3 and 4.

maximum revenue to be obtained from B than C (that is, $R_b^* > R_c^*$), A will attempt to form a coalition with C. In order to do so, however, he may need to pay C more than R_b^* (if $R_b^* < \frac{1}{2}R_a^*$, for example), and A will therefore have to pay some positive tax himself.

Because of the revolving cycles and the general distributional indeterminacy involved here, it is difficult to specify exactly what the expected income will be for each group over the long electoral sequence. However, we can make certain general remarks. First, unlike the case of unrestricted majoritarianism, differential productivity, thrift, and so forth will exercise some influence on the expected distribution because the minimal income that each will receive when in the minority can be expected to reflect basic income-earning capability. There is, then, some substantive meaning here in the notion that some are richer than others. Second, and as in the unrestricted case, the effect of government transfer activity seems likely to be in the direction of equalizing *expected* incomes. In general, we expect the maximum revenue obtainable from any group to be positively related to the tax-free income of that group. If so, the amount the poorest can expect to receive in transfers will exceed the amount the richest can expect to receive as transfers in absolute terms (and hence a fortiori as a proportion of pretax total income). The net effect is to condense the distribution of expected income over the long electoral sequence, but not to equalize it. In this sense, unrestricted majoritarianism generates *expected* income that is closer to equality; on the other hand, at each point in the electoral sequence, the observed distribution of income will be more nearly equal in the presence of the tax restriction than in its absence. And, of course, the aggregate of incomes will be predictably higher.

2. Uniform proportional income tax

We now add to the previous tax restrictions the requirement that taxes be uniform across taxpayers. Under this restriction, the majority must face the same tax rate on money income that the minority faces. However, since there are no restrictions on the use of tax revenues, the majority will rationally appropriate all tax revenues for itself; no transfer at all will be paid to the minority. Accordingly, there will still be cycling in this case. No particular majority coalition will be intrinsically stable, for any outcome can always be confronted with another that is preferred by two of the three individuals.

If it were not for the presence of excess burden in the tax system, this case would not differ from unrestricted majoritarianism. Uniform nondistorting taxes would be imposed by the majority so as to appropriate *all* the income of each individual. Revenues would then be divided in some proportions strictly among majority coalition members. In other words, the requirement of tax uniformity, in the absence of distortions within the tax system, does not constrain outcomes in any way. But because the tax system does distort — because it imposes an excess burden on majority members that increases at the margin with the tax rate — the majority will not rationally push the tax rate to its maximum revenue limits. Rather, the majority coalition will push taxes to the point where the cost to itself of the marginal dollar raised, including the excess burden imposed on majority members, is exactly one dollar. It is relatively simple to see that this will imply taxation at a rate lower than that required to generate maximum revenue from the minority. Specifically, let us consider tax-rate increases in the neighborhood of that maximum revenue level. An increase in the tax rate adds only a small amount to the net revenue collected from the minority (and hence to the net transfer received by the majority members) but adds substantially to the excess burden of taxation that majority members themselves face.

Specifically, the cost to individual i of raising an additional dollar of revenue consists of two elements: the individual's share of the tax revenue and the marginal excess burden he faces. That is, $C_i = r_i + (dW_i/dR)$, where r_i is i's share in the marginal dollar of tax revenue raised. Under a proportional money income tax, r_i is simply the ratio of i's money income to aggregate money income. It is clear that dW_i/dR tends to infinity as we approach the revenue maximum, because dR becomes zero at the maximum revenue level. Therefore, the marginal cost to i of an additional dollar of transfer also rises to infinity at maximum revenue. If each majority member shares equally in the tax proceeds (that is, each majority group receives half of each dollar of revenue received), each group will desire a tax rate at which C_i takes the value $\frac{1}{2}$.

Since r_i is larger for those with larger money incomes, and given that money income and total income are positively related, tax rates will be predictably lower when the rich are in the majority coalition than when the poor are. The poor therefore will lose relatively less when in the minority than the rich will lose when in the minority. Furthermore, although tax *rates* will in general be lower than in the nonuniform case, aggregate revenue will tend to be higher than in the nonuniform case since all must pay taxes. This means in turn that gross transfers will be larger.

In summary, the poor will tend to do rather better under the uniformity restriction: They will receive larger transfers on average than in the nonuniform case when in the majority and pay lower taxes when in the minority. The requirement of tax uniformity works in favor of greater redistribution *on average* and yet toward smaller variation over the long electoral sequence in the fortunes of any individual. The richest can do less well and the poorest less badly over the electoral cycle.

This is an important result and merits some emphasis. The requirement of tax uniformity in the presence of majority rule (without any corresponding uniformity restrictions on the transfer side) leads to a more equitable outcome, both in terms of expected income and in terms of the outcome at any point in the electoral cycle, than emerges in the absence of the uniformity requirement.

3. Uniform proportional income tax plus demogrant

Consider now the case in which uniformity restrictions are imposed on both the tax and the transfer side of the budget. The transfer uniformity is taken to require that revenues be divided equally among all citizens, in the form of an individual payment to all. Each group therefore receives thirty-three cents of each dollar of tax revenue raised. Uniformity on the tax side is defined, as in the preceding section, to involve a proportional income tax levied at the same flat rate on all individuals.

Given these restrictions, there will be some desired tax rate for each individual. This rate will be lower for any individual the higher his income, because he will be contributing a higher pro rata share of any dollar of tax revenue raised. In fact, any individual with income above the average will desire a zero tax rate − and hence a zero demogrant. Such an individual will contribute to revenue raised in proportion to his share of national income and will receive in return a per capita share enduring a net loss. Obversely, an individual with less than average income will desire a positive tax rate, one at which the cost to him of raising an additional dollar of revenue, including the marginal excess burden, will be equal to his per capita share of one-third. Clearly, the lower the individual's income, the higher will be the desired tax rate (and concomitantly tax revenue and demogrant). Here we have *no* cycles. Preferences over the single parameter t can be arrayed along a single spectrum, and majority rule will lead to the median income earner, in this case B, being decisive in determining the tax rate to be applied. There is no scope for a decisive coalition between A and C, because given the restrictions on taxes and transfers there is no arrangement that will make both A and C better off: A wants lower tax rates, C higher ones. Hence, the tax rate levied will be the tax rate desired by the median-income individual. As we have indicated, only if income of the median-income earner is less than average will he desire positive transfers; and he will desire more transfers the lower his income is. The extent of redistribution will depend, therefore, on the extent to which the income distribution is skewed toward the lower end.

In contrast with the earlier cases, then, the pattern of transfers in this case is entirely determinate and emerges identically at every point in the electoral sequence. The extent of such redistribution depends solely on the difference between mean and median income. Whereas the focus of normative analysis is on the *variance* of the income distribution, or some equivalent measure of inequality, the extent of redistribution under majority rule, so restricted, depends solely on the degree of *skewness*. In other words, majority rule, with uniformity restrictions on both tax and transfer sides, serves to connect redistribution to the wrong parameter. Changes in the distribution of income that are essentially irrelevant to redistributive ethics can generate substantial changes in the pattern of political transfers, whereas changes in the income distribution that are of considerable normative significance may leave the extent of transfers from rich to poor either unchanged or alter them in a "perverse" direction. Some simple comparative static results from our three-person analysis suffice to support these claims. Suppose, for example, that the income of the poorest falls, ceteris paribus. Then average income will by definition also fall. Median income will remain unchanged, however, so the extent of transfers will *fall*. Obversely, if the income of the poorest rises, ceteris paribus, transfers will rise. Consider, on the other hand, an increase in median income, ceteris paribus. In this case, transfers will fall, even though the relative share of the poorest in the total pie has declined. Of course, *some* changes in the income distribution will generate changes in the transfer pattern that are consistent with the dictates of distributive justice as conventionally interpreted. For example, as the income of the richest increases or decreases, ceteris paribus, the level of transfers will rise or fall. But as we have shown, the simple median voter model does not generate patterns of political redistribution that are an appropriate expression of what distributive justice requires.

VI. Direct constitutionalism and distributive justice

The central message of the institutional incidence analysis undertaken in the previous two sections is that ordinary majoritarian politics is a highly imperfect mechanism for securing distributive justice − at least as distributive justice is normally conceived. Two types of problems seem to be associated with majority rule. The first is one of distributional indeterminacy. The implementation of political transfers will always be such that the direction of transfer is away from the minority and toward the decisive majority, and the poorest cannot be expected to be in the decisive majority any more often than anyone else. Therefore, although the poorest can expect to be net beneficiaries of the political roulette wheel in the long run, the fact that political transfers will regularly flow in a perverse direction is one to be reckoned with. Exactly how one should evaluate a sequence of sytematically variable distributional outcomes is not a question to which social philosophers or normative policy analysts have given much attention. Nonetheless, it should be clear that without some answer to this question majoritarian institutions cannot generally be evaluated in terms of criteria for distributive justice. Is an income stream that varies randomly over time as "just" as a stream that yields income equally in each period? If not − and specifically, if the constant stream is to be preferred − there seems a good prima facie case for restricting majority rule in some way to produce, if possible, more stable distributional outcomes.

One way of restricting majority rule to achieve a determinate distribution is to require uniform proportional taxes and disbursement of revenues on an equal per capita basis. If such restrictions are imposed, however, a second problem with majority rule emerges: The transfer pattern generated will be insensitive to ethically relevant considerations. Specifically, the level of transfers will be perversely responsive to changes in the level of income of the poorest. Indeed, there is no guarantee that transfers will occur. Any transfers that do occur, of course, will be such as to benefit the poorest most of all. This is a direct concomitant of the restrictions imposed − that taxes be levied in proportion to income and that revenues be paid on an equal per capita basis. Nevertheless, majority rule does not seem capable of determining a *level* of transfers that is ethically appropriate or sensitive to the relevant parameters of the distribution.

It may, of course, be argued that the highly austere model of political process used in the foregoing sections is so remote from "real-world democracy" that nothing of any relevance can be concluded. Though fully conceding the starkness of the simple majoritarian model used, we reject the criticism. The object is to investigate the nature of the pressures on distributional outcomes that arise from electoral processes. Those pressures necessarily reflect the nature of the institutional setting, of which electoral competition under simple majority rule is a major (and many would argue predominant) feature. The danger of less formal treatment of democratic institutions is that one can become captivated by the prevailing political religion. There is, of course, much *talk* of distributive justice in the political rhetoric. The substantive issue is whether there is any reason to believe that distributive justice will be secured.

Given the simple model of majority rule we have developed, the answer is at best equivocal. Majority rule may be able to secure a more equitable outcome in the income distribution and may do so at tolerable cost. Majority rule, however, seems likely to work much better in this respect if constrained by the requirement of uniform proportional taxation. Such a requirement promotes more equitable outcomes in that it restricts the advantages to a decisive coalition of richer individuals in organizing large-scale transfers toward themselves, while restricting to a lesser extent the analogous advantages for the poorer. In all such cases, however, because transfers flow often enough in the "wrong" direction, the cost of securing any net redistribution in an expected sense is rather high — and seemingly unnecessarily so. For example, in cases 1 and 2 of Section V, it seems likely that all parties would receive larger returns if there were an agreement to secure the average distributional outcome at every point in the electoral sequence. This could also be construed to have purely distributional advantages. In a Rawlsian maximin setting, where no individual knows to which group he will belong, an arrangement that generates the expected distribution at every point has the advantage of entirely precluding the outcome in which the poorest are the exploited minority. Given the maximin criterion, this characteristic would seem to be decisive.

Might, then, some directly *constitutional* transfer arrangement be distributionally superior? If, in some quasi-Rawlsian setting behind the veil of ignorance at the constitutional level, individuals can be presumed to have well-defined preferences in relation to future income distributions and to transfer policies that might be implemented to constrain those distributions, why not seek to institute those policies at the *constitutional* level? Suppose, for example, that a uniform proportional tax rate is to be levied and that the resultant revenues are to be expended in equal per capita grants. Also suppose, however, that the tax rate (and hence grant level) were not determined by the median voter under majority rule but, instead, the tax rate (or the grant level) were selected *constitutionally*. Transfer policy would cease to be a matter for in-period political determination; the pattern of government grants would, instead, be part of the rules of the game.

There are four points to be made about such an arrangement. First, and somewhat surprisingly, the demogrant system is not necessarily as efficient a means of achieving a given *expected* distributional outcome as the uniform tax alternative examined in Section V.2. That is, reductions in the variance of the poorest's income stream over the electoral cycle are achieved at some loss in aggregate income. The reason for this seems to be that requiring transfers to be paid to all individuals increases the total revenue requirement of the transfer level that the poorest insists on when in the decisive coalition, and does so sufficiently to offset the disadvantages to the poor when in the minority. Recall that in the model discussed in Section V.2, tax rates are lower when there is a coalition of the richest than when there is a coalition of the poorest, so the disadvantages to the poor from being in the minority are already somewhat moderated. In any event, to achieve the same expected income for the poorest via a demogrant system does require a higher tax rate and hence larger excess burdens than in the case where transfers are restricted to majority members, even though the poorest will be in the exploited minority some of the time.

Second, and on the other side of the ledger, the constitutional demogrant system obliterates incentives to expend resources in an attempt to ensure that one is part of the decisive coalition, incentives that exist whenever majoritarian cycles prevail. If political rent seeking of this type is at all large (which, as we have already argued, it could very well be), then the lower excess burdens on the tax side in a majoritarian system restricted only by the requirement of uniform proportional taxes may well be more than offset. In this event, efficiency considerations favor the explicit constitutional transfer package.

Third, although it seems natural to refer to such an arrangement as "constitutionally determined *transfer*," there is something rather misleading about such terminology. There is, after all, no sense in which these policies would "redistribute" resources or income among persons. Rather, the constitutional order would involve a set of property rights in which each individual genuinely "owned" only a portion of the product that the labor embodied in his person generated. On the other hand, each would own an equal share of some portion of the product that the labor embodied in other persons generated. The government could not be taken to be *transferring* income from the rich to the poor — by virtue of gratuitous altruism, hatred of the rich, or any other aspect of "Robin Hoodism." The arrangement would simply be part of the institutional structure under which individuals' basic property rights were defined and enforced. In fact, this is perhaps not so different from current institutional arrangements in Western democracies. Citizens do, by virtue of the prevailing powers of the state, make claims on the personal productivity of other individuals – claims the state legitimizes and effects through the tax-transfer system. The crucial difference between what is here suggested and what currently prevails is that under the constitutional alternative, the claims individuals make on one another under state aegis would be *uncontingent*, not varying according to fluctuating electoral fortune. The rights that citizens possessed by virtue of such constitutional arrangement of taxes and transfers would then be no different from other things they could properly construe as *owning*. At this point, notions of distributive justice and formal justice (as examined in Chapter 7) overlap. Because distributive justice considerations are applied to the rules rather than merely to outcomes, and because these considerations are endorsed and applied under constitutional consensus, the outcomes emergent under rules satisfy the requirements of "distributive justice," whatever the characteristics of the distribution of income those outcomes may exhibit at any given time.

Finally, once it is recognized that criteria of distributive justice are applicable to the choice among rules rather than some imagined choice among imaginable distributional outcomes, one cannot simply presume that the set of rules most conducive to distributive justice will be ones that "transfer" income. It is certain that economists generally approach the issue of redistributive policy with a strong predilection for cash transfers as the most efficient form of securing desired distributions. But this proposition may not be true once the domain of discourse shifts from selection of the desired *distribution* toward the institutional structure from which desirable distributions may emerge.

There could be all sorts of rule changes that promoted greater equity in the pattern of emergent outcomes. In basketball, for example, we could diminish the natural advantages of tall players either by raising the height of the basket by five feet or by attempting to handicap tall players explicitly in some way (say, by weighting goals scored by the inverse of the height of the scorer). It is not obvious that the latter scheme would be more just, in any acceptable meaning. In the same way, rule changes in social affairs need not involve explicit redistribution through political process to secure more equitable outcomes. In light of our analysis of transfer patterns under simple majority rule, it would hardly be surprising if more efficient routes to distributive justice could be found.

VII.   Summary

The central object of this chapter has been to examine the question of distributive justice through constitutional eyes. Our point of departure has been the observation that the "benevolent despot" model of political processes is totally inadequate for the purposes of discussing distributive justice, just as it is in other pieces of normative social analysis. We cannot adequately characterize governments as "choosing" among alternative distributions. Rather, distributions emerge from the complex interaction of autonomous agents, all making individual choices under a given set of rules. The evaluation of alternative distributions is to be seen as a preliminary step only, as a piece of abstract normative theorizing, which of itself is incapable of revealing anything at all about policy-relevant matters. What is required is an examination of the way changes in the rules under which individuals interact change the pattern of distributive outcomes. Such examination we call "institutional incidence analysis."

The analytic core of this chapter contains just such an institutional incidence analysis for an extremely simple model of majority rule. We make alternative assumptions about the excess burdens generated by taxes and transfers and examine the distributional effects of imposing various restrictions on the ways taxes can be levied and transfers paid. The general conclusion to be derived from this analysis is that majority rule is at best a highly imperfect means of pursuing distributive justice. Majority rule either generates cycles (that is, is basically distributionally indeterminate) or, when appropriately restricted, generates a specific pattern of transfers that is perversely responsive to normatively relevant changes (say, to changes in the income of the poorest).

All this suggests the possibility of lifting the determination of the redistributive or transfer budget out of the jurisdiction of in-period majoritarian politics and making it a matter of explicit constitutional compact. This can, of course, be done. But a constitutional decision to embed some transfer operations in the general rules of the game cannot be presumed. Expected effects on the distribution of income will presumably be relevant in the choice among alternative sets of rules, and rules generating more nearly equal patterns of distribution may, ceteris paribus, be preferred. Chosen rules, however, need not involve "handicapping" the more successful players. There is available, at the constitutional level, a wider set of options, and the means chosen for achieving more equitable outcomes need not necessarily involve interpersonal transfers.

The analysis here, to be sure, falls short of being definitive. It does, we believe, nevertheless point in the right direction. Traditional discussions of distributive justice are hopelessly remote from the real world of distributive politics. Indeed, crucial political constraints are typically ignored altogether, and the institutional feasibility of distributive justice is brushed aside as an irritating minor technicality. This may be an acceptable procedure for the moral philosopher, but for the social analyst it is totally inadequate. Our object here has been to expose that inadequacy and to indicate the sort of inquiry required to fill the void.

For present purposes, it seems clear that faith in the capacity of ordinary majoritarian processes to generate equitable patterns of distribution is naive indeed. In the absence of rules designed to restrict the operation of majoritarianism in particular ways, almost anything goes. Equality in an *expected* sense emerges only because of the intrinsic unpredictability of the future pattern of political coalitions, and what remains to be distributed in the world of "politics without rules" cannot be anything but small.

CHAPTER 9

Is constitutional revolution possible in democracy?

I.   Introduction

This book is an extended essay in persuasion. We have tried to offer logical bases for imposing constraining rules on the political actions of persons, including ourselves, as present or potential actors in political roles. We hope that our arguments for the desirability of accepting a "constitutional attitude" have been convincing, both in the abstract analysis and in the practical applications of this analysis. Widespread acceptance of such an attitude is a prerequisite of genuine constitutional reform. We would, however, be naïve in the extreme if we failed to acknowledge major barriers to the achievement of any shift in the basic rules of political order. This chapter is devoted exclusively to analysis and discussion of these barriers.

It is, we presume, evident that we must answer the question of the chapter's title affirmatively. If we did not, the discourse of this book, and of much of our work elsewhere, would have to have been driven by purely aesthetic purpose. In one sense, we share a moral obligation to hold fast to the faith that persons organized in a polity can reform the rules by which and under which they live. Any other belief, it seems to us, would be a counsel of despair. This faith in the potential for reform must, nonetheless, be distinguished from constructive analysis of the difficulties of escaping the dilemmas we confront. If analysis of these difficulties were to yield wholly negative results, faith in any potential for reform might be sorely shaken. We need, if at all possible, to present a scenario in which genuine constitutional change takes place through the activities of men and women we can all recognize. If people were saints or angels, the dilemmas we face would never have emerged in the first place.

We should also emphasize the relevance of the last two words in this chapter's title. We examine prospects for constitutional revolution *in democracy*, which means not only that our attention is limited to democratic polities but, more important, that constitutional change is required to be "democratic" in the sense that it must emerge from the internal workings of politics in which the whole electorate potentially participates, rather than from the dictates of certain "divinely qualified" persons either within or outside the community. We use the phrase "divinely qualified" here because any discrimination among persons with respect to the formation of the basic rules of social order must be legitimated by reference to some external supraindividualistic criterion.

This limit to our analysis excludes from consideration all nondemocratic revolutions, constitutional or otherwise. Such revolutions are always possible, even in countries that have long been accustomed to democratic procedures of governance. A group of persons – a military junta, a single party leadership, a ruling committee, an elitist establishment – seizes power and imposes its will on all persons outside the dominating group. It is relatively easy to model constitutional–institutional reform in this fashion, which amounts to saying that it is easy to play at being God. The academic scholar-scientist, in particular, may be tempted to play such a role by imagining that he holds the revolutionary reins of power. In this dream world, the scholar-scientist can make his own idealized suggestions for constitutional change while still under the guise of participation in an ongoing dialogue with his fellows.

The issue we face is much more difficult than that involved in playing God. Our concern is with the prospect of securing *general agreement* on changes in the basic rules of the political game, even on the part of persons and groups who seem to be relatively advantaged under existing institutional arrangements. In other terms, our concern is with prospects for noncoercive and voluntary resolution of the generalized social dilemma that seems to describe modern politics. Honest diagnoses suggest that the dilemma is real, and throughout this book, we have taken these results to be stipulated.[1] We do not live in the best of all possible constitutional worlds, and here we examine the possibility of escaping into a different one.

II. Pareto-superior change and Wicksellian unanimity

We shall begin by making a summary detour through some fundamental principles of theoretical welfare economics, specifically through the Paretian criterion for the justification of a change or move. Pareto

---

[1] For earlier, related analyses that were more diagnostic, see James M. Buchanan, *The Limits of Liberty* (University of Chicago Press, 1975); also see Gordon Tullock, *The Social Dilemma* (Blacksburg: Center for Study of Public Choice, Virginia Polytechnic Institute, 1974).

supplied a classification scheme, in which all possible social "situations," "positions," or "states" belong to one of two mutually exclusive sets. The first set includes all nonoptimal, or inefficient, positions; the second includes all optimal, or efficient, positions. The latter set consists of all nondominated positions, with dominance being defined for all persons in the relevant community.[2] No change can be made from a *Pareto-optimal* position to any other position without at least one person in the community being harmed. A *nonoptimal* position is one from which some change can be made in such a fashion that at least one person is benefited and no one is harmed. This purely definitional classification scheme then allows us to say, formally, that there must exist at least one position within the Pareto-optimal set that can be attained by change from any position in the nonoptimal set, a change that will harm no one. Such a change is defined as *Pareto superior*.

At this purely formal level, we need not be concerned about the precise meaning of a "social state," "position," or "situation." In the orthodoxy of modern welfare economics, a "social state" has been defined almost exclusively in terms of an imputation (allocation or distribution) of endowments and/or goods among persons. Needless to say, such an outcome, or end-state, usage of the Pareto criterion is inappropriate for our purposes in this book and elsewhere, but this concluding chapter is clearly not the place for an extended critique of end-state methodology. In this discussion, the Pareto criterion is applicable to rules, or institutional arrangements within which persons act to generate patterns of outcomes.

Saying, then, that a generalized social dilemma exists amounts to classifying the existing rules of the socioeconomic—political game as nonoptimal, or inefficient. And if we insist on noncoercive and voluntary agreement, we restrict "efficient" or "optimal" to the Pareto meaning. This tells us, in turn, that if our diagnosis of the presence of a dilemma is correct, there must be Pareto-superior changes that are possible. If the rules are nonoptimal, there must be reforms that will benefit everyone.

If we translate the formal Pareto scheme into Wicksellian terms, we can say that if a genuine dilemma exists, it must be conceptually possible to make some change on which *all* persons in the community could agree. Unanimous agreement on some proposed change in the rules must be at least conceptually possible. Critics might immediately

[2] For what is perhaps the most concise statement of the Pareto classification scheme, see Ragnar Frisch, "On Welfare Theory and Pareto Regions," *International Economic Papers*, 9 (London: Macmillan, 1959), pp. 39–92.

suggest that unanimous agreement smacks of utopian absurdity, at least in terms of practicable implementation. In our view, however, criticism of this sort amounts to putting things the wrong way around. The relevance and applicability of the Wicksellian−Paretian criterion as a benchmark on which analysis and discussion of constructive constitutional reform must be based are in no way challenged by such criticism. If we are consistent in our determination to limit analysis to prospects for internal change, for "democratic" reform of political arrangements, there is no alternative criterion for the evaluation of proposals.

III.   Distributional limits and prospective rules

There are obvious limits on the range of possible Paretian−Wicksellian changes from any defined status quo. This point can be seen most clearly if we shift to the more orthodox setting and define the status quo position as an imputation of valued goods among separate persons in the community. To the extent that a proposed change involves a purely distributional shift, it cannot be classified as Pareto superior, even as a conceptual possibility, if "goods" are defined to include all that persons value. (Of course, if the distribution were defined in terms of physically measurable commodities, Pareto-superior changes might be made.) If we think of some value-numeraire, any change from an initial distribution must reduce value for at least one person, whose agreement could then never be secured. That is to say, if a proposed change involves "taking away" valued goods from some person or persons and "giving to" others, the change could never be accepted voluntarily by those who would be harmed in the process.

A direct implication of this elementary point is that constitutional revolution, in the sense discussed here, would be impossible in a democracy if this revolution were conceived as a fundamental shift in the distribution of commonly valued goods and services or in the distribution of claims to such goods and services.

This distributional restriction on the scope of constitutional change may initially seem quite severe. This impression is misleading, however, and tends to be fostered by the total absence of realism in the definition of any status quo position as *a* distribution of goods. It is necessary to keep in mind that our concern is not with potential changes in specific end states, or outcomes, even if such changes were within the realm of the possible. If the relative positions of individuals in sociopolitical order are described by an imputation of valued goods, services, and claims, distributional *re*allocation must characterize any change. (No one would expect poker players to divvy up the chips after the game had been played.) Our focus is rather on the potential for changes in the *rules* or institutions of social order. These rules provide the framework within which patterns of distributional end states emerge from the interaction of persons (players) who play various complex functional roles. The precise distributional effects of a change in the rules on any identified person or group at any point in time may be difficult if not impossible to predict. A status quo defined only in terms of the rules (the laws and institutions) within which persons act is conceptually very different from a status quo described by a particular distribution of valued goods and claims. (The poker players may all agree on a change in the rules for future play, regardless of the rules under which play has proceeded during earlier rounds of the game.)

Let us digress, briefly, by noting that the proclivity of mathematical economists to force all analysis into mathematically tractable forms has done serious damage to clarity of thought with respect to the end state–rules distinction. It has proved relatively easy, mathematically, to define distributions of goods in vector language. But how could a status quo be described mathematically if what exists is a set of rules that constrain but do not determine individual choices that, in turn, generate patterns of distributional outcomes? End states lend themselves to mathematical manipulation; processes do not.

Changes in rules are *prospective* in their distributional implications, whereas changes in observed distributions themselves are necessarily *retrospective*, with reference to the choice behavior of the persons who act to generate the results. Changes in rules that can lay any claim at all to consensual agreement can, at best, modify personal expectations about future distributional patterns. Rule changes cannot modify observed distributions as such, unless, of course, such changes are applied ex post facto.

An example of the distinction is provided by normative tax theory. A collective decision to levy a progressive tax on incomes is a change in fiscal rules. Despite the distributional consequences that might be predicted, such a decision may conceptually be agreed to by all persons in the community, particularly if there is a time lag between the agreement and actual levying of the tax. An individual would know that if he chose to earn income, this income would be taxed at progressive rates. But contrast this with a collective decision to levy a tax on wealth. In this case, persons who have accumulated wealth have made prior choices under other rules. A change in fiscal rules of this sort violates all criteria of "fairness" and could never lay claim to Pareto superiority, even as satisfying a purely conceptual criterion.

Acknowledgment of the prospective nature of any change in rules that qualifies as Pareto superior carries important implications for the design of proposals for reform. To the extent that proposed changes in rules explicitly embody time lags between approval and implementation, the ability of persons who are potentially affected to predict with accuracy the impact on their own identifiable positions must be reduced. Prospective rules introduce uncertainty into the calculus of those who participate in the decision making, and this uncertainty increases with the length of the time lags.

The temporal element becomes even more significant when it involves the *duration* or *permanence* of the proposed rules change. To the extent that persons who must choose among rules do so in either the knowledge or the expectation that any alternative, once chosen, is to remain in effect over an extended sequence of periods, they will be less able to predict how particular rules will affect their relative positions over the same sequence. The logical basis of the differentiation between the decision rule for making changes in the constitution (amendment procedures) and the decision rule for making choices within given constitutional rules lies in the recognition of this temporal distinction.

Proposals for changes in rules that are known to be or expected to be short-lived, even if adopted, are more predictable with respect to their distributional impacts. Hence, agreement on short-lived change may be more difficult to secure. Indeed, the meaning of "rule" implies quasi-permanence; a game whose rules were changed with every round of play would be little different from a game without any rules.[3]

In their book *The Calculus of Consent* (1962), James Buchanan and Gordon Tullock used the prospectiveness and permanence properties of constitutional rules as the essential means by which an individual can construct a bridge, of sorts, between short-term, identifiable private interest and long-term, nonidentifiable self-interest, which then becomes "public interest."

The construction has a close affinity to the somewhat more familiar Rawlsian veil of ignorance.[4] In the Rawlsian framework, the individual has a moral obligation to choose among principles of justice as if he were behind a veil of ignorance. And at a different level of analysis, the stance so depicted is held to describe empirically widely held notions

[3] For a careful and comprehensive treatment of the significance of time lags in a constitutional calculus, see Antonio Pinto Barbosa, "The Constitutional Approach to the Fiscal Process: An Inquiry into Some Logical Foundations" (Ph.D diss., Virginia Polytechnic Institute and State University, 1975).

[4] John Rawls, *A Theory of Justice* (Cambridge, Mass.: Harvard University Press, 1971).

about justice. That is to say, persons "should" try to adopt the veil-of-ignorance position, and, furthermore, persons do embody some such a stance when they seriously consider, and talk about, basic rules for sociopolitical order. The Buchanan–Tullock derivation is, in comparison with the Rawlsian, less demanding on individuals in that, at least in the limit, they are forced by the circumstances of the choice setting to adopt a stance that is equivalent to the veil of ignorance. Because of the inherent uncertainties about their own positions, persons must, on rational self-interest grounds, use criteria akin to the fairness precepts outlined by Rawls. The effect of uncertainty is to mitigate substantially any purely distributional aspects of genuine constitutional choice.

IV.   Status quo entitlements and distributional envy

A second major hurdle to be surmounted in generating consensus on basic constitutional reform is indirectly related to the distributional aspects discussed in Section III and, in one respect, exists precisely because the requisite limits of distributional uncertainty cannot be attained. Realistically, we must recognize that persons will not, and cannot, make constitutional choices behind a veil of complete ignorance, owing either to their inabilities to adopt the moral stance urged on them by John Rawls or to the impossibility of designing institutional circumstances sufficient to make such a stance rational on strict self-interest grounds. To some residual extent, distributional implications of any proposed change in rules can be predicted, including the prediction of differential impacts on identifiable individuals and groups. This fact alone would seem to stymie consensual constitutional reform from the start. Must the question posed in this chapter's title be answered negatively?

This barrier to potential agreement is not nearly as serious as it may at first seem. The necessary presence of some predictable distributional impact of any proposal for change will thwart general agreement on any simple version of the proposal. But at this point it is useful to recall the earlier detour into Paretian–Wicksellian welfare analytics. If the status quo set of rules is, indeed, nonoptimal, or inefficient, there must exist potential agreement on *some* change in structure. The working out of such an agreement, even for conceptual evaluative purposes, may, however, require a complex network that includes various compromises, side payments, compensations, bribes, exchanges, trade-offs – a network aimed precisely at offsetting the predictable adverse distributional properties of the proposed changes. If particular persons, as individuals or as members of groups in the economy, foresee distributional harm as a result of the implementation of a simple change in the rules, the designer-proposers must work out additional elements of a "package deal" that will change the results.

The problem here is not one of difficulty in locating the necessary elements of a complex constitutional "exchange" that will promise net benefits, ex ante, to all participants. There may be many such packages that would command general assent, especially when there are major overall gains to be made by a change in institutional–constitutional structure. The discovery of such mutually beneficial proposals, best considered as complex exchange propositions, is the proper task of the specialist in political economy.[5] The problem worthy of our attention here concerns the willingness of those who may be direct beneficiaries of structural change to pay the compensations that may be required to secure general agreement.

The problem can be stated differently. All parties in the political community may be unwilling to accept the status quo distribution of entitlements generated under the operation of existing rules. This distribution of entitlements may not be acceptable to many persons as the appropriate starting point from which genuine constitutional reform is to be made. That is to say, there may be no way to get from "here" to "there" until prior agreement is reached on the "here" and the embodied distribution of rights that exist.

Consider land reform in a developing country as an example (and purely as an example, since we make no claim to competence in the analysis of comparative efficiencies of alternative institutional arrangements in such situations). Let us stipulate that there is general agreement among all persons in the community that land reform will increase the overall efficiency of the national economy, efficiency being objectively measured in dollars of gross national output or product. From this fact, it would seem to follow that some reform proposal, in a complex package deal, could be worked out on which everyone could be brought to agree. Such a proposal would have to include compensation to existing owners of extensive landholdings that would be sufficient to secure their acquiescence to a change in ownership patterns. To finance such compensation payments, however, prospective landholders and/or taxpayers generally would have to sacrifice some pur-

---

[5] See James M. Buchanan, "Positive Economics, Welfare Economics, and Political Economy," *Journal of Law and Economics* 2 (October 1959): 124–38; reprinted in James M. Buchanan, *Fiscal Theory and Political Economy* (Chapel Hill: University of North Carolina Press, 1960), pp. 105–24.

chasing power, some share of their net promised benefits. This result might seem less desirable to these groups than the result achieved by a simple "taking" of the landed estates. Despite the acknowledged net gains from the land reform, persons who themselves would be in the net beneficiary groups might remain unwilling to finance the necessary payments to existing landowners, on the grounds that status quo holdings are "unjust." This attitude, and behavior stemming from it, might prevent any consensus from being reached on constitutional change, even with the widespread knowledge that such a change would generate major overall efficiency gains.

The prevalence of such an attitude toward patterns of holdings, or rights, in the status quo will, of course, depend in part on the individually estimated prospects for successful alternative avenues through which change can be implemented. Respect for the status quo distribution of entitlements and, hence, willingess to pay the compensation required to attain consensus on change depend critically on whether the allegedly "unjust" entitlements and claims can be changed *without* the voluntary agreement of existing holders of such entitlements being obtained. The temptation to confiscate privately held capital values overtly through the exercise of power by dominating political coalitions is always present.

Perhaps even more important, the expected value of gains from politically orchestrated "taking" may remain positive, and differentially higher than the expected gains from genuine constitutional change, for many persons who are not at the time, but may expect to be, members of political coalitions capable of carrying out confiscatory action. Indeed, the problem discussed here may be most extreme in those situations in which "political property rights" are most uncertain.

In our land reform example, many persons may consider existing holdings to be "unjust" and hence appropriately subject to overt confiscation (to nondemocratic constitutional change in the terms of our reference in this chapter), but at the same time these persons may be uncertain as to their own potential voice in governmental–political decisions. Despite this uncertainty, however, they may be unwilling to support any scheme that will allow some politically orchestrated "buy out" of existing holdings. The situation of the nominal owners of the estates in the status quo may be similar even if on the other side of the issue. If these nominal owners acknowledge their impotence in the face of identifiable opposition coalitions, they might voluntarily agree to structural rearrangements that include much lower net compensation than straightforward market-value estimates might produce. On the other hand, if these holders maintain confidence in their power to influence political outcomes, they may demand compensation in excess of what other members of the political community will finance, especially given the estimated threat potential that members of the second group think they possess. The impasse that may arise in such settings is analogous to the problem that arises in market transactions when ownership rights to potentially tradable goods are not well defined and legally protected.[6]

The land reform example should not be taken for more than that, an example. Many other examples, such as slavery in the American South in the 1850s, might have been selected. The central point is that ambiguity and uncertainty about the distribution of political rights under a set of constitutional rules may inhibit or even totally prevent changes in these rules, despite a general acknowledgment that such changes would improve welfare. Nondemocratic change in the form of violent revolution or civil war might become the alternative to consensual reform in such settings.

The barrier to genuine constitutional reform analyzed in this section varies in significance with the perceived "legitimacy" and "effectiveness" of the existing political constitution, the status quo set of rules. To the extent that this constitution commands little respect, in part because it is seen to fail in its function of limiting the scope of both governmental and private intrusions into what are widely held to be protected spheres of activity, the direct-confiscation alternative to Pareto-superior or consensual change may seem to offer higher present value to most citizens. The somewhat ironic result is that it may be much easier for a country to achieve genuine constitutional revolution if its citizenry has long adhered to a "constitutional attitude," fostered by a historical record during which limits on the power of governments have proved effective at least to a degree. If there has been a widely acknowledged separation between "law" and "legislation," to use Hayek's terminology,[7] or between "constitutional" and "postconstitutional" – "in-period" choices, or between "changes in rules" and "play within defined rules," the willingness of persons to seek somewhat different and more inclusive processes of decision making to change rules, as opposed to processes for political action within existing arrangements, is increased. Conversely, it may be difficult to achieve basic constitutional change in a political setting where governments are seen to have

---

[6] For a discussion of this point, see James M. Buchanan, *The Limits of Liberty* (University of Chicago Press, 1975). ch. 2.

[7] F. A. Hayek, *Law, Legislation and Liberty*, 3 vols. (University of Chicago Press, 1973, 1976, 1979).

been effectively unlimited in power and authority. Why should an unlimited majority coalition, either existing or potential, ever seek constitutional change through consensus when the same results can be achieved at lower cost?

In these respects, it would presumably be easier for the United States, or any political structure characterized by an effective division of power, to effect changes in its political structure than it would be for the United Kingdom or any parliamentary democracy in which political authority is concentrated in a single legislative assembly.

V.   Constitutional change and free riders

The barriers to constitutional reform discussed in Sections III and IV are significant. We should not underestimate either the distributional implications of any change in structure, with their feedback effects on potential consensus, or the effects of uncertainties in the political status quo. Nonetheless, it could be argued that these barriers to reform are less important than the one to be discussed in this section, one that is much more difficult to supersede in any normatively predictive sense.

We refer to the general problem of "publicness," in the formal welfare-economics meaning of the term, and to the behavioral implications of this characteristic, which are often summarized under the rubric "free rider." In its most comprehensive forms the question is, How is "public good" produced? How is "public bad" avoided? How is collective action motivated other than via the private interests of individuals?

It is relatively easy to conceptualize or model a small group of players in an ongoing game considering possible changes in the rules of play, the rules that describe the game itself. But what is the analogue in the larger, more comprehensive sociopolitical "game" in which there are literally millions of players? Who are to take upon themselves the personal burden of designing provisional proposals for basic changes in the rules when the promised benefits accrue *publicly*, that is, to all members of the political community, and with no differentially identifiable residual claims to the promised "social" profits? What is the constitutional equivalent of the patent law, which guarantees a special, even if limited, monopoly privilege to the inventor and which, in turn, offers incentives for creative effort by all potential inventors? What is the political−constitutional equivalent of entrepreneurial profits, the search for which drives the economy and motivates attempts to locate higher-valued ways of organizing production and combining resources, both within and across markets, broadly defined?

Can general rules be changed in a deliberative process of collective choice, even if there are acknowledged possibilities of Pareto-superior reforms? And if not through deliberative choice, how can general rules be modified? Must we resign ourselves to the acceptance of one of what seem to be only two alternatives? Must we acknowledge that changes in basic institutions can be imposed only nondemocratically, by a group seeking to promote its own interests, the alternative avenue of "reform" that we have refused to discuss in this chapter? Or failing conscious constitutional change and eschewing nondemocratic "reform," must we fall back on slow, unconscious, and unintended processes of social–cultural evolution, with little more than pious hope that such changes as do occur will lead us toward rather than away from a set of arrangements that might be conceptually evaluated to be Pareto optimal?

Confronted with questions like these, the economist seems likely either to despair or to avoid relevant thought altogether by playing mathematical games. An economic model of behavior that lays any claim at all to predictive power must rely on the uniformity of human nature summarized in *Homo economicus*, or economic self-interest objectively defined. Such a model of behavior has served economists well; the model in all its variations explains much of what we know about the political–governmental sphere of human action in addition to the much more that we know and can explain about human action in market relationships. This economic model yields meaningful predictions; testable hypotheses can be derived about the organization and functioning of political parties, coalitions, committees, pressure groups, governmental agencies, and legislatures. Hypotheses about how bureaucrats behave, how budgets are constructed, how regulation operates — these and others emerge from application of the central *Homo economicus* postulate. But all such hypotheses rest, finally, on the explanatory power of this self-interest motivational assumption. The professional economist must look at the governmental–political process as driven by the same forces that drive the market process; even when analysis incorporates the recognition that self-interested behavior is not nearly so amenable to simple modeling in political as in market choice.

It should be evident, however, that the basic analytics of "positive public choice" cannot be readily extended to explain changes in the basic rules of political order that are necessarily "public" in scope. The individual actor in the positive public-choice model does not act contrary to his defined self-interest, even if it is not so easily defined as some of the simplistic exercises might suggest. To the extent that "investment" in institutional analysis, design, argument, dialogue, discussion, and persuasion is costly in a personal sense, the individual of the orthodox model will forgo such investment in favor of more immediate gratification of privately directed desires. Why should anyone do "good"? There is no way that economists who stay within the strict limits of the discipline can respond to such a question; they cannot manipulate utility-maximizing actors so as to offer a satisfying response.

VI.   The role of norms

Economists have great difficulty in moving beyond the rather simplistic, if powerful, models of human behavior grounded in self-interest motivation. We claim no exception to this generalization about our disciplinary peers. Nonetheless, anyone who diagnoses the plight of modern democracy in terms of the existence of a social dilemma described by a set of nonoptimal rules must give up in despair, become a revolutionary, or go beyond the models of utility maximization, nontautologically defined. To hold out hope for reform in the basic rules describing the sociopolitical game, we must introduce elements that violate the self-interest postulate.

If persons do not behave in accordance with their own economic self-interest, objectively defined and measured, on what basis do they act? The hard-nosed positive economist mounts an effective critique of peers in the other social sciences and in social philosophy when they are challenged to produce an alternative model with predictive content. The economist is well equipped to recognize mush for what it is, and when noneconomists hypothesize that persons want to "do good," he quickly detects the absence of predictive content. To make such hypotheses operational, even at the level of analytic discourse, additional definition is necessary. What, precisely, do persons do when they "do good"? If individuals differ widely in their conceptions of "good," attempts by each to "do good" amount to little more than random deviations from behavior modeled on self-interest postulates.

If the alternative hypotheses are to carry predictive weight, they must be amended to state something like the following: "People want to do good or to take right actions, and they share a single conception of what is good or right." The *commonality* of the norm, at least over a large number of persons, is a necessary feature of any operationally useful theory of choice or action that moves beyond the strict individualistic models.[8]

---

[8] We are indebted to David Levy for calling our attention to this point. See his paper "Towards a Neo-Aristotelian Theory of Politics: A Positive Account of Fairness" (Center for Study of Public Choice, Virginia Polytechnic Institute, December 1981, mimeographed).

Applied to the problem at hand, which is that of deriving some conceptual explanation of why individuals might be expected to seek out, design, argue for, and support changes in the general rules of the sociopolitical order when, by presumption, such behavior would be contrary to identifiable self-interest, it is necessary to resort to some version of "general interest" or "public interest" as the embodiment of a shared moral norm. That is to say, persons must be alleged to place positive private value on "public good" for the whole community of persons, over and beyond the value placed on their own individualized or partitioned shares.[9] Furthermore, this "public good" that is privately valued must be that state of affairs defined by the interaction of freely choosing individuals, rather than some transcendental notion derived from God or Karl Marx.

If, however, individuals do, indeed, place a positive value on the shared conception of "public good," the economist-critic can then ask the straightforward question, How could a community made up of such persons ever find itself in the social dilemma that has been diagnosed? Why would a community of such persons ever need a change in the rules of the game, or why is there a need for any rules at all? The appropriate response is equally straightforward. To hypothesize that persons place positive value on a shared "public good," defined as indicated, does not in itself imply anything at all about this evaluation relative to that placed on the furtherance of individuals' private economic interests. The economists' explanatory model reasserts itself at this point and suggests the presence of a necessary trade-off between "public good" and "private good" in the choice calculus of any person who maximizes utility. From this elementary point it follows that the observed degree of "public regardingness" in behavior will depend on the relative costs as these emerge in the institutional setting.

It is precisely here in the argument, or so it seems to us, that a categorical distinction must be made between choices confronted within or under an existing set of rules and choices confronted among alternative sets of rules themselves. In the first of these two settings, that of postconstitutional or in-period choice, the relative costs of choosing courses of action that further the shared "public good" may simply be too high, relative to the increment in "public good" promised to result from such action, to shift behavior significantly away from economic

---

[9] Howard Margolis has attempted to formalize such a model. His difficulties in so doing illustrate the magnitude of the task. See his *Selfishness, Altruism and Rationality* (Cambridge University Press, 1982).

self-interest. In the second choice setting, by contrast, the costs of furthering "public good" may be significantly lower, so much so that the same person who behaves in accordance with narrowly defined self-interest within the given set of rules may well behave in accordance with precepts of shared norms when making genuinely constitutional choices.

The categorical difference here stems from the meaning of *general rules*, the generality referring to their application to all members of the body politic. The principle is an elementary one in theoretical welfare economics and in the theory of public finance, and it has been widely recognized, especially since it was emphasized by Baumol in *Welfare Economics and the Theory of the State*.[10] Nonetheless, the principle is often overlooked in otherwise sophisticated discussion. A good example is the discussion of public and private charity. Many who have opposed governmental transfer programs refer to the opportunity persons have, in their private capacities, to make charitable transfers to the needy. These critics then go on to infer that arguments in support of governmental transfer programs must arise from a desire to impose coercive taxation on those who would not voluntarily make charitable transfers. Some such motivation is probably present in many of the arguments, but these critics overlook the distinction made here to the effect that persons may, in a collective setting in which their actions are generalized, voluntarily agree to transfer schemes that involve costs to them that would never be borne in a private institutional situation. An individual might voluntarily agree to a tax-transfer scheme that imposes a net individual cost of one hundred dollars, if he knows that all other, similarly situated persons will also bear net costs of one hundred dollars each. The same individual, however, may contribute only fifty dollars, or less, to privately organized schemes having the same purpose in the absence of the political program.

The nature of rules changes ensures that all persons in the political community will be involved similarly, at least in one meaning of the term. (All players are required to play by the same rules, whether these rules are those that now exist or those that might exist after a change.) In considerations of proposals for a change in the rules, therefore, there is much less conflict between what can be called "private" and what can be called "public" advantage. An individual cannot, in nearly so direct a sense, set off his own private gain against public gain as he might do in purely private market choice or in political choice made

---

[10] William J. Baumal, *Welfare Economics and the Theory of the State* (Cambridge, Mass.: Harvard University Press, 1952).

within ordinary majoritarian institutions for decision making. In either of the latter two decision settings, the behavior of a person in generating "public bad" or in failing to produce "public good" might be motivated strictly by the opportunity to secure private gain. Such an opportunity might not really exist, at least directly, in the genuinely constitutional-choice setting.

The free-rider dilemma that emerges in constitutional choice is of a sort quite different from what enters the choice settings just noted. In constitutional choice, free ridership refers largely to the potential absence of individualized interest in general rules rather than to the presence of any directly contrasting nongeneral or private interest, where nongenerality itself ensures the differentiality. As we have noted, some such identifiable private interest may remain in any constitutional choice; it may not be possible to design proposals for constitutional change that will place persons behind sufficiently thick veils of uncertainty. Nonetheless, a shared moral norm in such a setting has much less "work to do" than it might in a nonconstitutional setting.

VII. Toward a civic religion

In this chapter, we have discussed three major barriers to constitutional reform in democratic social order. The thrust of our argument has been that these barriers can be overcome. We do not, however, underestimate the task Western democracies face, and we do not want to seem unduly optimistic. We are asking no less than that the basic rules of the socioeconomic–political game be changed, rules that have been in place for decades, and that these changes be made peacefully while the game continues to be played under the old rules. This order is a tall one indeed, and we should be under no delusion that a constitutional revolution will simply emerge, in revolutionary fashion, without a conscious investment of effort.[11]

Our efforts, in this book and elsewhere, are aimed largely at the academic constituency, at our peers in the social sciences, law, and philosophy. And it is here that we must begin, especially if we accept Keynes's dictum about the influence of academic scribblers. It is naïve to think that practicing politicians and practical individuals become constitutional statesmen without some coherent set of ideas provided by academe, either before or along with political articulation.

---

[11] In our opinion, great damage has been and is being done by modern economists who argue, indirectly, that basic institutional change will somehow spontaneously evolve in the direction of structural efficiency.

The first step is the achievement of some measure of academic consensus on diagnosis. We must come to agree that democratic societies, as they now operate, will self-destruct, perhaps slowly but nonetheless surely, unless the rules of the political game are changed. In the United States in particular, there seem to be modest grounds for hoping that such a consensus is in the process of construction, notably with respect to the fiscal and monetary rules, which have been the subject of much discussion in the 1970s and 1980s. There is increasing awareness that something other than ordinary politics will be required to generate fiscal and monetary discipline, that a regime is needed that will function in the acknowledged long-term interests of all participants in the body politic. The search for, and discussion of, alternative fiscal and monetary rules has begun.

In more general terms, this book is an expression of the hope that a new "civic religion" is on the way to being born, a civic religion that will return, in part, to the skepticism of the eighteenth century concerning politics and government and that, quite naturally, will concentrate our attention on the *rules that constrain governments* rather than on innovations that justify ever expanding political intrusions into the lives of citizens. Our normative role, as social philosophers, is to shape this civic religion, surely a challenge sufficient to us all.

We must redesign our rules, and our thinking about rules, with the ultimate aim of limiting the harm that governments can do, while preserving the range of beneficial governmental−collective activities. We plead with our fellow academicians to cease their proffering of advice to this or that government or politician in office. Good games depend on good rules more than they depend on good players. Fortunately for us all, and provided that we understand the reason of rules in the first place, it is always easier to secure agreement on a set of rules than to secure agreement on who is or is not our favorite player.

Index

151